INFLATION
AS A
GLOBAL
PROBLEM

INFLATION AS A GLOBAL PROBLEM

Edited by RANDALL HINSHAW

THE JOHNS HOPKINS UNIVERSITY PRESS
BALTIMORE AND LONDON

Manufactured in the United States of America

The Johns Hopkins University Press, Baltimore, Maryland 21218
The Johns Hopkins University Press Ltd., London

Library of Congress Catalog Card Number 72-8903
ISBN 0-8018-1447-2

Library of Congress Cataloging in Publication data
will be found on the last printed page of this book.

CONTENTS

v

CONTRIBUTORS

SVEN W. ARNDT, Fellow, Crown College, University of California, Santa Cruz

RICHARD BLACKHURST, Professor of Economics, Johns Hopkins Bologna Center

ARTHUR I. BLOOMFIELD, Professor of Economics, University of Pennsylvania

ARNOLD COLLERY, Chairman, Department of Economics, Amherst College

MARCELLO DE CECCO, Professor of Economics, University of Siena

GORDON K. DOUGLASS, Chairman, Department of Economics, Pomona College

JOHN EXTER, Senior Vice President, First National City Bank of New York

J. MARCUS FLEMING, Deputy Director, Department of Research, International Monetary Fund

GOTTFRIED HABERLER, Galen L. Stone Professor of International Trade, Harvard University

Sir ROY HARROD, Oxford University

RANDALL HINSHAW, Professor of Economics, Claremont Graduate School

CONRAD C. JAMISON, Vice President and Economist, Security Pacific National Bank

FRITZ MACHLUP, Walker Professor of Economics and International Finance, Princeton University

GIOVANNI MAGNIFICO, London Representative, Banca d'Italia

H. C. McCLELLAN, Assistant Secretary of Commerce for International Affairs, 1955–57

ROBERT A. MUNDELL, Professor of Economics, University of Chicago

ROBERT T. PARRY, Vice President, Security Pacific National Bank

GARDNER PATTERSON, Assistant Director General, General Agreement on Tariffs and Trade (GATT)

GISELE PODBIELSKI, Visiting Professor of Economics, Johns Hopkins
    Bologna Center
Lord ROBBINS, Chairman, Court of Governors, London School of Econom-
    ics
Sir ERIC ROLL, Director, Bank of England; Director, S. C. Warburg & Co.,
    Ltd.
JACQUES RUEFF, Chancellor, Institut de France
WALTER S. SALANT, Senior Fellow, The Brookings Institution
WILSON SCHMIDT, Deputy Assistant Secretary of the Treasury
LEONARD S. SILK, Editorial Board, New York Times
ALEXANDER SWOBODA, Professor of Economics, Graduate Institute of
    International Studies, Geneva
WILLARD L. THORP, Assistant Secretary of State for Economic Affairs,
    1947–52
ROBERT TRIFFIN, Frederick William Beinecke Professor of Economics,
    Yale University
JOHN PARKE YOUNG, Former Chief, Division of International Finance,
    U.S. Department of State

FOREWORD

This is the report of the third Bologna-Claremont conference on
international monetary problems, held in Bologna, Italy, April
15-18, 1971, under the auspices of the Johns Hopkins Bologna
Center, in cooperation with Claremont Graduate School. The
theme was "International Aspects of the Problem of Inflation."
The order of priorities in the discussions at these conferences over
the five-year period they span—from "Monetary Reform and the
Price of Gold" in January 1967, to "Problems of International
Adjustment" in March 1969, to the problems of worldwide inflation in the spring of 1971—reflected the major issues in the steadily
growing crisis which was to reach a climax in President Nixon's
world-shaking decisions of August 1971. What is recorded in the
resulting three volumes is therefore a chronicle of the deep and
growing concern of some of the West's most distinguished economists and of their reflections on what might be done to cope with
some of the most serious and complex international problems of
the contemporary world.

The conference organization followed the creative pattern set at
the first conference in 1967. Lord Robbins, as on that occasion,
introduced the subject with characteristic lucidity, profundity, and
objectivity, and the meeting thereafter pursued its course under
the wise and skillful chairmanship of Willard L. Thorp. The spon-
taneity and informality of the discussions is conveyed in the text
of this volume, edited by Professor Randall Hinshaw, who shaped

the substantive plans for all three conferences and served as rapporteur with incomparable skill.

The Bologna Center is deeply indebted to the International Foundation of New York, which made an initial substantial grant for the conference, thus assuring additional support from other contributors; to the Haynes Foundation of southern California for its assistance with the travel expenses of several California participants, no less than for the moral support of the Bologna-Claremont conference program in general, reflected in the attendance at the conference of its chairman of the board, Francis H. Lindley; to the Banca Commerciale Italiana and, personally, to its president, Dr. Raffaele Mattioli, for very generous financial assistance; and to the Banca d'Italia for its very kind and helpful contribution.

The success of every conference—and this was an unusually successful one—is in no small measure due to the inconspicuous, painstaking, dedicated labor of its supporting staff, in this case, the staff of the Bologna Center. Everyone gave unsparingly of his time and effort, from Trudi Pellegrini, the director's secretary and Francis Gordon-Cooper, the Center's bursar, both of whom have from long experience become almost professional managers of conference affairs, to the custodian, Angelo Buldini, who quietly and efficiently handled logistical problems, and to Antonio Poltroniere, who performed the very responsible task of supervising the recording of all the conference discussions. Sincerest thanks are due to all of these and to many others unnamed who helped in less conspicuous but scarcely less important ways.

C. GROVE HAINES
Director
The Bologna Center

I. INTRODUCTION

Randall Hinshaw

This book is a scenario of a conference on "world inflation" which took place at the Johns Hopkins Center in Bologna, Italy, in mid-April 1971. The conference, in which some of the world's foremost international monetary authorities participated, was the third in a biennial series jointly sponsored by The Johns Hopkins University and Claremont Graduate School, each conference reflecting an intensive effort to probe as deeply as possible into the international monetary problem which appeared to be most important at the time the meeting took place.[1]

The theme of the 1971 Bologna conference was inflation as a global problem. In the past, inflation has generally been thought of as a national problem, and there have been innumerable cases of national inflation, or even of "hyperinflation," unaccompanied by inflationary tendencies in the rest of the world. But the present inflation has in recent years become a worldwide phenomenon— a situation without precedent in the past century except during and immediately after World Wars I and II.

The conference was recorded on tape. Under the expert chairmanship of Willard L. Thorp, the first three sessions concentrated on questions of diagnosis and the remaining two on ques-

---

[1] A book resulted from each of the first two conferences. The first, *Monetary Reform and the Price of Gold: Alternative Approaches*, appeared in 1967, and the second, *The Economics of International Adjustment*, in 1971. The books were published by The Johns Hopkins Press and were edited by Randall Hinshaw.

tions of therapy. In a brief introduction, it would be presumptuous, as well as entirely superfluous, to attempt a summary of the dialogue—a task admirably performed by Lord Robbins at the final session. Instead, with the advantage of a slightly later view of the problem, I shall comment briefly on a few broad issues which seem to me of special significance.

The first, in the field of diagnosis, concerns the role of the United States in global inflation. This is a controversial matter on which it is difficult for economists on either side of the Atlantic to be completely objective. But as an American who spent half of 1971 in Europe, I shall try. My first observation would be that, in that year of crisis—with the dollar under continuous heavy pressure because of a staggering U.S. payments deficit; with President Nixon in mid-August suspending dollar convertibility into gold, introducing price and wage controls, and in December agreeing to dollar devaluation—it would be difficult for any observer, however biased, to doubt that the United States, a country accounting for well over a third of the Western world's output, was playing the leading role in the generation of world inflation. If only because of its importance in the world economy, the United States was the principal culprit.

At the same time, it should be pointed out that the global character of the present inflation did not become apparent until the late 1960s. During the early 1960s, price levels were stable in many countries, including notably the United States. Indeed, the U.S. price level has never been more stable than it was at that time; beginning with the year 1958, the wholesale-price level, on a 1958 base, rounded to a figure of 100 for seven years in a row!

Nor is there any convincing evidence that the United States was "exporting" inflation during these years. As Professor Machlup pointed out in his highly informative opening statement, monetary expansion in the United States during the period 1948–67 was the lowest of any of the ten industrial countries he studied, averaging only 2.4 percent a year. And the competitive position of the United States during the early 1960s is reflected in the fact that exports of goods and services greatly exceeded imports; even if exports financed by U.S. Government grants are excluded, the export surplus (including services) amounted to $6.7 billion in 1964 and to $5.3 billion as late as 1965.

But there was a fly in the ointment. The remarkably stable price level and the impressive competitive position were accompanied by substantial unemployment. For the years 1958 through 1964, unemployment hovered between 5 and 7 percent of the civilian labor force, the average being just under 6 percent. In a bold effort to deal with this problem, President Kennedy proposed extensive federal tax reductions in January 1963. These were not enacted until February 1964 under President Johnson, but the tax cuts, plus the escalation of the Vietnam war in 1965, were followed by a sharp decline in unemployment, the rate dropping steadily from 5.7 percent in 1963 to a low of 3.5 percent in 1969—in other words, to an employment performance considerably better than the 4 percent target frequently cited in the early 1960s as a realistic definition of "full" employment.

Unfortunately—though not surprisingly—the stimulation of the American economy was accompanied by a departure from the fine record of price stability achieved in the period 1958-64. The price rise was slow at first but gathered momentum, becoming particularly disturbing in the sector of consumer prices, which rose by 5.4 percent in 1969 and by 5.9 percent in 1970—a rate at which the consumer price level would double every twelve years.

Whether one leans toward a "monetarist" or toward a "cost-push" explanation of this price behavior, both forces clearly were at work. The rise in the price level was certainly encouraged by sharply increased monetary expansion; from an average annual growth rate of 2.4 percent for the period 1948-67, the U.S. money supply (currency plus demand deposits) suddenly grew by 7.1 percent in 1968 and by 6.0 percent in 1969. At the same time, the cost-push element in forcing prices upward is clearly reflected in the fact that hourly wage rates in recent years have increased much more sharply than output per man-hour. In this connection, it is instructive to compare the five-year period 1966-70 with the seven-year period 1959-65. In the earlier period, output per man-hour in U.S. manufacturing actually rose at a higher average annual rate (4.0 percent) than hourly earnings in manufacturing (3.1 percent). In the later period, however, the situation was dramatically reversed, with output per man-hour rising at an average annual rate of only 2.2 percent and hourly earnings rising at an average annual rate of 5.2 percent.

Alarmed by the accelerating inflation, the Johnson administration in 1968 introduced a 10 percent surtax on individual and corporate incomes, and made sharp cuts in federal expenditure on space research, community development, housing, and education. Restrictive fiscal policies were continued by the Nixon administration, the federal budget in 1969 showing the first calendar-year surplus since 1960. These measures appeared to accomplish little more than a rapid retreat from full employment. By 1971, unemployment—at 5.9 percent—was at the highest annual level in a decade, and inflation was still very much under way. If any evidence were needed that inflation was continuing at a vigorous pace, one had only to look at what was happening to U.S. merchandise imports, which increased by 14 percent in 1971. Normally, imports rise moderately each year in response to the steady growth in the national income; for the fourteen-year period 1952–65, the average annual increase was 5.1 percent.[2] But when prices are tending to rise more rapidly at home than abroad, one of the ways in which the long-suffering consumer can make his money go farther is by switching from domestic to foreign sources of supply. One of the first signals of serious inflation in the United States was a 20 percent increase in merchandise imports from 1965 to 1966, with an even bigger spurt in 1968, when imports increased by 23 percent over the 1967 level.

As Professor Machlup showed in his opening statement, the U.S. inflation has been accompanied by a sharp acceleration in inflationary tendencies abroad, reflected both in sharply increased monetary expansion and in briskly rising prices. From the late 1960s onward, one can speak of inflation as a world problem. How much this acceleration of inflationary pressures has been due to the inflation taking place in the United States is a matter of judgment, but there is no doubt in my mind that, given the international monetary setting, developments in the United States have been mainly responsible. Under a regime of fixed exchange rates, price increases in one part of the world are rapidly communicated to the rest of the world. Moreover, as several conference members pointed out, the world has for many years been, in effect, on a "dollar

[2]This period excludes both the abnormal early postwar years, dominated by European recovery and the Korean War, and the post-1965 years of brisk inflation in the United States.

standard," which means, among other things, that the chronic deficits in the U.S. balance of payments have been largely "settled" in dollars, the dollars providing the basis for monetary expansion in other countries. The dollar standard does not explain all the recent monetary expansion going on outside the United States, since some countries have been vigorously inflating their money supplies by purely domestic methods, but there can be no doubt that the enormous international flows of dollars in the late 1960s and early 1970s have been an important source of inflationary pressure abroad.

These foreign-owned dollars, held in the form of bank balances in the United States and U.S. government securities, grew from a total of $21 billion at the end of 1960 to a total of $43 billion at the end of 1970. Under the shattering impact of an unprecedented U.S. payments deficit, they increased by another $19 billion in the first ten months of 1971—to a total of $62 billion.

But this is only part of the story. Supplementing the foreign-owned dollars just referred to has been the extremely rapid growth since 1960 of "Eurodollars"—dollar balances held, not in the United States, but in European banks, notably in London. Eurodollar deposits, which to their holders have all the attributes of money, grew from a total of $3 billion or so in 1960 to a total of $56 billion at the end of 1969. During the year 1968 alone, they grew by 46 percent, and during 1969 they grew by another 71 percent. No serious discussion of the problem of global inflation could ignore the mushrooming of this complex and completely unplanned phenomenon, which Professor Machlup aptly described as "stateless money," and a highly illuminating session was entirely devoted to the subject.

In addition to questions of diagnosis, the conference was very much concerned with the implications for policy. Here the prescriptions fell into two broad categories: international measures and domestic measures. On the international side, the dollar standard was generally regarded as a major culprit in the generation of global inflation, and there were those—notably Jacques Rueff, Robert Triffin, and John Parke Young—whose major concern was reform of the international monetary system. Short of reform, it was pointed out by Lord Robbins and Fritz Machlup that countries which were more successful than others in maintaining internal price stability could resist external inflationary pressures by appreciating their currencies. In the month following the conference, this prescription was applied by Austria, The Netherlands, and Switzerland.

Generating considerably more controversy were questions of domestic policy. Here attention was focused on the United States, because of its dominant position in the Western economy. The conference discussion was strongly influenced by an exasperating feature of the U.S. inflation, namely, the coexistence of inflation with substantial unemployment. Inflation and unemployment are strange bedfellows, and pose a problem not readily amenable to either classical or Keynesian remedies, since measures designed to arrest inflation are likely to increase unemployment, while measures designed to reduce unemployment are likely to increase inflation. If evidence were needed, ample experience is available, as recorded earlier, from the bitter frustrations of the Johnson and Nixon administrations in attempting to deal with this dilemma.

With the two goals of full employment and price stability both keenly in mind, Sir Roy Harrod strongly recommended an "incomes policy" for the United States, under which increases in wage rates would be limited to increases in output per man-hour. In Sir Roy's view, recent inflation in the United States and in the United Kingdom has been of the cost-push variety, and he was convinced that the only way to achieve both full employment and price stability under such conditions would be by applying Keynesian policies in an environment in which government would prohibit excessive wage increases. Harrod's remarks led to a lively dialogue as well as to an extended statement by Lord Robbins in his closing address. Opinion on incomes policy was sharply divided, with critics stressing the administrative and political difficulties. Since the Harrod approach was adopted by President Nixon less than four months after the conference took place, the dialogue on this topic—in many ways prophetic—makes particularly interesting reading.

Radically different was the highly original prescription presented by Professor Mundell. Although as concerned as Sir Roy with the goals of full employment and price stability, Mundell took the position that these goals could be simultaneously attained through an appropriate "mix" of fiscal policy and monetary policy. His views met with considerable resistance around the conference table. I found them highly intriguing and, having the unfair advantage of additional time to reflect upon them, I will take this opportunity to present my reactions to what might be called Mundell's "$50 billion idea." For it makes a great deal of difference whether he is right or wrong.

First a word of background. In both classical and Keynesian thinking, fiscal and monetary policy are generally regarded as properly operating in the same direction, inflation calling for fiscal and monetary restraint, and unemployment calling for fiscal and monetary ease. But what should fiscal and monetary policies be in a situation where brisk inflation and widespread unemployment are occurring simultaneously? If these policies are used in the same direction, then one is resigned to the melancholy prospect of a "trade-off" between inflation and unemployment—the familiar trade-off revealed in the famous "Phillips curve," about which much was said at the conference. But if the two types of policy can be used in opposite directions, with one promoting full employment and the other promoting price stability, the picture clearly becomes much brighter. And this is exactly what Mundell proposes.

Mundell's basic insight is that, with a given money supply, a trend toward unemployment can actually be inflationary. A fall in employment means a fall in the aggregate supply of goods and services, and therefore—other things being equal—a trend toward higher prices. An increase in employment, on the other hand, means an increase in the aggregate supply of goods and services, and thus, with a given money supply, a trend toward lower prices.

On these grounds, Mundell was highly critical of both the Johnson and Nixon policies of fiscal restraint. The stated purpose of the higher federal taxes and the selectively reduced federal expenditures (both actually initiated under President Johnson) was to check U.S. inflation, and spokesmen for the Nixon administration candidly admitted that, in their thinking, a certain degree of unemployment was an unfortunate but necessary part of the process. Mundell argued eloquently that this induced unemployment, far from tending to curb the inflation, actually tended to increase it; and the historical record appears to be entirely consistent with this contention.

The U.S. policy mix during the late 1960s was one of fiscal restraint and monetary ease. Under the conditions of 1971, Mundell argued that it should be exactly the reverse. To curb inflation—and, in particular, to curb inflationary expectations—the rate of monetary expansion should be held down to a low level; and to reduce unemployment, federal taxes on personal and corporate incomes should be sharply reduced as a means of encouraging an increase in consumption and investment. Under the Mundell doctrine, any increase in employment—in an environment of monetary restraint—would itself have an anti-inflationary effect by increasing the aggregate supply of goods and services.

There is clearly a great deal which can and should be said about this ingenious prescription, and much of it was said at the conference. Here I shall limit myself to two observations.

In the first place, a policy of monetary restraint and fiscal ease means that budget deficits must be financed in a way which does not conflict with that policy. The Mundell program implies an increased budget deficit, at least initially, and if unwanted monetary expansion is to be avoided, the necessary government borrowing must come from noninflationary sources, notably from private and corporate saving. This could mean a higher level of nominal interest rates, though here much would depend on expectations. If lenders were convinced that the new policies would bring greater price stability, they might well be content with a lower "inflation premium"; under such conditions, a stationary or even slightly lower nominal interest rate would be consistent with a higher real interest rate (nominal rate corrected for price-level changes). Of course, for the Mundell program to result in an increase in employment, the funds borrowed by the government should not be funds that would otherwise be spent on consumption or investment. At the same time, it should be borne in mind that, to the extent that the program were actually successful in increasing employment, tax revenues—despite the tax cuts—would begin to increase, and the need for government to borrow might decline or even disappear.

In the second place, perhaps the most important advantage of the Mundell prescription would be the possibility of substituting tax reduction for excessive wage increases. From a worker's standpoint, it should be a matter of indifference whether he receives a given increase in "disposable income" in the form of a wage increase or in the form of a tax reduction. But it makes a great deal of difference to the economy. In the former case, the cost structure is clearly raised, introducing the danger of cost-push; in the latter case, the cost structure is completely unaffected. In the fight against the sinister combination of unemployment and inflation, surely a useful area for the exercise of ingenuity would be the development of employee tax benefits as a substitute for wage increases—in particular, for wage increases in excess of the growth in output per man-hour.

But now to the conference itself. Except for the introduction, the book is an unabridged transcription of the conference tape recording. Editing has been minimal. Under the skillful organization of Chairman Thorp, the conference discussion falls neatly into eight chapters, all presented in chronological order. Chapter II contains the opening address of the moderator, Lord Robbins, who in his inimitable way established the high intellectual tone which pervaded the entire meeting. In Chapter III, Fritz Machlup, in a remarkably able and compact statement, provided a wealth of statistical background and analysis on the conference theme. Five eminent authorities—Gottfried Haberler, Sir Roy Harrod, Robert A. Mundell, Jacques Rueff, and Robert Triffin—were invited in advance to contribute ten-minute statements on issues relating to global inflation, and their views are presented in Chapter IV, which is followed by a general dialogue on the issues in Chapter V. Of notable interest is Chapter VI, which is devoted to a highly informative exchange of views on the significance of the Eurodollar market in world inflation—an exchange in which several noted authorities on this market participated. Chapters VII and VIII are concerned with questions of therapy; the former is a dialogue, led by Sir Roy Harrod, on incomes policy as a remedy for cost-push inflation, and the latter is an exchange of opinion, led by Professor Mundell, on the role of fiscal and monetary policy in coping with the painful combination of inflation and unemployment. The final chapter begins with Lord Robbins's admirable summary of the conference discussion, and ends with an international monetary blueprint for the future by John Parke Young.

II. INFLATION: AN INTERNATIONAL PROBLEM

Lord Robbins

Chairman WILLARD L. THORP: This is the third international
monetary conference of our wandering Bologna-Claremont group.
At each of our previous conferences, the problem of inflation, although not explicitly on the agenda, has played a role. In his opening statement at the first meeting in 1967, Lord Robbins pointed
out that, although early postwar attention was centered on the fear
of deflation, Sir Ralph Hawtrey had predicted in 1944 that inflation would be the actual postwar problem and Lord Keynes had
remarked that Hawtrey might be right. Bernstein gave a brief historical analysis relating inflation and deflation in the past to the
uneven growth of the world gold supply, and regarded this growth
as so fortuitous as almost inevitably to lead to perennial bouts with
either inflation or deflation. Rueff and Emminger argued that the
gold-exchange standard had opened the door to inflationary effects
in the past, and there were several members, including Dr. Emminger, who argued against increasing the price of gold because
they feared that such a move would bring on inflation. So I would
say that, at our first conference, inflation appeared largely as a
possible danger—something to worry about, but not such an immi-
nent threat as to call for international action.

That meeting was in January 1967 here in Bologna. At our second conference in California in March 1969, inflation received
more attention. In Hinshaw's book presenting the final report of
that conference, there are seven references to inflation in the in-

dex, whereas in his report on the first gathering, there are only three. In discussing the balance of payments, various members referred to the part played by price levels, and it was the American price level which was of major concern. Indeed, some members, such as Randolph Burgess, felt that international adjustment—the theme of the conference—would cease to be a serious world problem if the United States were able to control its inflation.

The conference actually concentrated on "crawling pegs," "wider bands," and other devices for exchange-rate adjustment. In the last analysis, inflation was regarded as a national event, and the international problems thus created were to be resolved by various forms of flexibility in the exchange rate. But at the end of the conference, Bernstein spoke of a world with an inflationary bias; he went so far as to refer to a world of "perpetual" inflation. Perpetual is perhaps too strong a word ever to be used in economics, but the sense of his remark was very clear. His feeling was that exchange rates were seldom adjusted upward; the usual move was downward, and thus the net impact throughout the world of exchange-rate changes was a perpetual tendency toward inflation.

Since the Claremont gathering of 1969, the problem of inflation has come into much greater prominence. We now think of inflation as a world problem, and that is why we are here today. The problem no longer seems to be simply a collection of isolated national phenomena but rather to be a world condition. As we have done before, we shall start our conference by going back to first principles, and I now call on our distinguished moderator, Lord Robbins, to introduce the subject.

Lord ROBBINS: The center of gravity of this conference is inflation as an international problem. Therefore the eventual focus of these opening remarks will be on specifically international matters. But I take it that it will not be out of order if I start with a few remarks on inflation in general. I do this, not because I think that there is anything particularly new to say at this level, but rather in order to make plain what I should regard as axioms of judgment and policy if there were no international complications.

I will not spend time at this stage dwelling on the facts of inflation; they will be the subject of presentation by the expert skill of Fritz Machlup, who sits next to me. But I think it is not inappropriate to begin with a few words on the effects of inflation in

general and the reasons why I personally regard them as undesirable.
I doubt whether I should have troubled to do so earlier in my life;
in those days, for the most part, professional opinion was hostile,
if not to all the results of unexpected inflation, at any rate to inflation as a principle of policy. But in recent years, I regret to say,
there have been some signs of a change in opinion. When I read one
of the leading economists of the Western world—no less a person
than Harry Johnson, a man for whose humanity and judgment I
have the warmest respect—saying that he doesn't mind inflation,
I feel that some explanation of why I do mind inflation is not
altogether superfluous.

I take it as incontestable that inflation alters the distribution of
wealth. How exactly it alters it depends, of course, on the nature
of the process. Demand inflation transfers wealth to those who
receive profits and perhaps to some groups of wage earners who
have the luck to get in first. In each case, however, the recipients
of incomes fixed in terms of money tend to suffer—universities
compelled to keep proportions of their assets in gilt-edged securities,
investors who are fools enough to listen to the exhortations of
governments to buy savings bonds, salaried persons whose emolu-
ments are reviewed only at long intervals, pensioners of all kinds—I
don't think it can be denied that much suffering and distress of
mind is caused to members of such classes by depreciation of the
value of money. Those members of the academic world who can
always raise extra money by work on the side may not be greatly
troubled. But that frame of mind depends very much on what part
of the academic world you're in. If you happen to be an Egyptolo-
gist or a life-long editor of some rare manuscript, you may suffer
distress comparable to that of the rest of the fixed-income population.

All this is brushed to one side by the contention that, properly
foreseen, these injustices can be eliminated. Now doubtless there
is something in this. Democratic politicians, at least, will not be
willing to lose too many votes at popular elections by leaving
those who are directly dependent upon them to languish forever
hopelessly behind the cost of living—though I have yet to learn of
any finance minister who had the same degree of compassion for
those from whom he, or his predecessors, borrowed with fulsome

appeals to their patriotism or their prudence. But I think that it
needs to be pointed out that, to the extent to which these distrib-
utive changes are compensated, then to that extent any positive
"benefit" from the inflation disappears. Indeed, and I'm surprised this needs to be said, if all the injustices of inflation were
anticipated and if they were all avoided by simultaneous compensation, the inflation would lose all its point—whatever that may
be. It would be equivalent simply to an alteration of the unit of
account, either by adding noughts to all the figures on coins and
in bank accounts and stock-market securities, or by changing,
to use David Hume's immortal analogy, from Arabic to Roman
numerals. Well, as those who are prepared to tolerate, or to bless,
inflation will be quick to point out, this will not happen. So we
can cheerfully sit back and say with Housman, although not in
his sense,

> Be still, be still, my soul: it is but for a season;
> Let us endure an hour and see injustice done.

But what about the effects on production?

Let me say at once that I can see no good at all in the effects of
cost inflation. Apart from the distortions of accountancy to which
I shall refer in a moment, it militates against investment and so
against economic growth. If you think that is beneficial—and, of
course, economic growth has its enemies—well and good; if not, then
the contrary. It is possible, I suppose, that some entrepreneurs may
be forced, quicker than would otherwise have been the case, to look
round for cost-saving inventions and to make a more economic
use of resources generally. But clearly this has very narrow limits
and, once the cost inflation exceeds a certain figure, is very unlikely
to go further. In any case, if it happens at all, I would say that
burning down the house to get roast pig was by comparison a
rational operation.

Where demand inflation is concerned, the position is certainly
different. Where the rate of inflation is comparatively small—say,
2 percent—then it is very likely that the increase of profits thus involved will, for a time at least, lead to a brisker use of resources
and perhaps to a somewhat greater rate of accumulation than
otherwise might have been the case. For those who trouble to read
any but the latest textbooks and journals, it will be realized that

this was well known to most of the classical and neoclassical econ-omists—it is splendidly set forth in John Stuart Mill's *Principles*—and was among the staple items of discussion of inflation following World War I.

But before we come to the conclusion that recognition of this possibility should lead us to lend positive approbation not only to the possible historical results of past inflations of the less violent order, but also to inflation as a positive policy for the future, there really are certain complications to be taken into account if we are not to write ourselves down as pure suckers. First, we should note that in order that the forced-saving process can be at all extensive, it is necessary that it should be unanticipated. Those inflations of the past when something of the sort may be conjectured to have taken place—the metallic inflations of the sixteenth and seventeenth centuries, for instance—came as something of a surprise to the peo-ple concerned: they did not know what was happening. But once falling monetary values are expected, people change their plans accordingly. Interest rates rise, contracts anticipate increased costs, and so on; and to the extent to which this takes place, so the allegedly beneficial effects diminish. In the end, if the stimulus is to be maintained, then the rate of inflation must increase so as to exceed the changed expectations. And this is, of course, one way in which inflation can become cumulative.

On top of this, we must note a further adverse effect which may be attributed to the naiveté of the accounting profession, accus-tomed to expect of governments the same integrity that they demand of themselves. The habit of estimating depreciation quotas which until recently has been customary in the English-speaking world, spells trouble for business in times of inflation. Provision for depreciation at constant prices is of course inadequate under such conditions. The result is that, as inflation proceeds, particularly if it is a cost inflation, the liquidity positions of corpo-rate enterprises become more and more difficult. This is perhaps why simple-minded businessmen who swear to government inquiries that their planning is seldom, if ever, affected by changes in interest rates, continue to raise their age-long howls of pro-test if money rates are raised in an effort to arrest the process of inflation.

Finally, in this connection, I cannot forbear to notice the moral and social effects of a period of more than very moderate inflation. I say nothing of the effects on public utilities and nationalized industries whose prices, being influenced by political considerations, are usually hopelessly behind the gun when costs are rising all round. But I do think it is worth emphasizing the general effects on commercial honesty and private morals produced by the anxieties of continually rising prices. When all is thus unstable, private behavior becomes a matter of *sauve qui peut*. Tax evasion, fraudulent selling, wild speculation in real estate become the order of the day. For anyone who has actually watched at close hand the effects of inflation in Latin America or in continental Europe after the two great wars of this century, it will take a great deal more persuasion than a few credulous bits of simplistic statistical analysis to make him believe that the atmosphere of the casino is favorable either to long-run economic growth or to the stability of political democracy.

It is time to come to the central subject of this conference—the international difficulties created by inflation, their causes and possible remedies.

Now from this point of view, as Professor Machlup doubtless will be telling you, the salient feature of what has been happening in recent years is the unevenness of the inflationary process. There have been rises in prices everywhere—declines in the purchasing power of the local currencies. But they have been at different rates and different orders of magnitude in different areas. If it were not so, if the fall in the value of money had been everywhere the same, there would be far less to discuss at this conference. We could still inquire what general causes were operative and what general measures might be adopted to arrest the movement—if by any chance we didn't happen to think it beneficial. But the complications arising from different rates of inflation in different areas, the difficulties in the foreign-exchange markets, the migrations of hot money, the possibilities of local insulation, the pathetic bewilderments of finance ministers and bankers as they fly from center to center to hand out bitter reproaches or desperate appeals for aid—these happenings would not come under our survey if the rate of inflation were uniform everywhere. But it is just these cases on which we must concentrate our attention.

Before doing this, however, there is a technical distinction which is quite fundamental to a correct judgment on these matters. Not all increases in local price levels and local incomes are to be regarded as inflationary in the sense in which general movements in a closed community or the world as a whole are to be so regarded. They *may* be inflationary; they may be due to increases of local expenditure unaccompanied by an increase in the real value of local production: most of the current world inflation has had its origin in such movements. But they may also be merely responses to favorable changes in the general conditions of international supply and demand; and, far from being inflationary, in the sense of financial movements serving no purposes save perhaps the transitory extraction of forced saving, in such cases they are an essential part of the equilibrating function of international capital movements.

Let me try to make my meaning clear. Consider for a moment certain possible movements within a closed economy where there is only one monetary system. Suppose that in a part of this economy there take place changes which involve changes in the relative value of products or factor services rendered in the area—a discovery, for instance, of valuable mineral resources, a changed fashion in tourism, or (what sometimes happens after periods of war or disorganization) an improvement of labor productivity in respect of articles in elastic international demand. Clearly, in such circumstances, we should expect a rise in money incomes in that area and, insofar as some products were not cheapened by the original cause of the movement, a corresponding rise in their prices. Would we call this inflation? Well, of course, this is a semantic question; words can mean what you like, but I should have thought that to call a movement of this sort inflationary was decidedly inconvenient and confusing. You only have to carry the thing to its limit and consider the rise of prices and the accompanying rise of incomes of a single industry, due to any of the causes I have mentioned, to see how very odd that would be.

Now exactly the same thing can occur in national areas which are parts of the world economy. If the demand for their product rises in comparison with the demand for the products of other areas, or if the volume of these products forthcoming in markets

of elastic demand increases, then, in a regime of fixed exchange
rates, the way in which the workers and owners of productive
resources situated there can receive the increased share of world
production which is awarded to them by the market is just this:
that domestic incomes and prices of home products rise *pari passu*,
and the increase of real incomes comes via increased power to buy
import goods, goods with import ingredients, or various kinds of
foreign services. This is a simple corollary of the Ricardian theory
of the distribution of the precious metals, as developed in our own
time by Taussig and other famous figures, and borne out by observation everywhere. And I would add that, if this sort of movement
does not take place, then, other things being equal, the banking
system of the area thus favorably affected will tend to accumulate
more and more of whatever assets are international media—gold,
dollars, or what you will. Movements of this sort therefore can be
conceived in a world in which the movements of price levels in the
world as a whole are not inflationary. And as I have already said,
they can in fact be regarded as a condition of international equilibrium rather than the reverse. To draw in gold or dollars as a result
of this type of influence and not to make it the basis of an increase
of money incomes would certainly be positively deflationary as regards the rest of the world. To describe such local rises in prices and
income therefore as inflationary—in the same way as one would describe upward movements of prices and incomes due to an excess
of domestic expenditure over domestic production and imports—
seems to me confusing in conception and likely to lead to wrong
notions of policy.

But the trouble is that not all inflows of funds from abroad are
just a natural response to an increased value of local production.
Some may be due to the fact that elsewhere there are taking place
genuinely inflationary movements of aggregate expenditure which
make adverse the balances of payments in the areas concerned and
make favorable the balances of payments of the more prudent
areas. And now a new problem arises for the financial authorities
in the areas favorably affected. In the earlier case—the case of the
favorable turn in the terms of trade—a monetary expansion was
simply a natural reflection of this improvement in the local position. But in the case I am now discussing—a favorable balance of
payments due to increases of expenditure elsewhere, unaccompa-

nied by increases in the real value of production—a local expansion is simply *the importation of other countries' unwarranted expansion*, and carries with it no such advantages. In this case, I should certainly describe the resulting increase of prices and incomes as an inflation; and I would urge that the effects on distribution and production would justly be described in those terms.

I hope I have said enough in this rather abstract discussion to establish a broad distinction both as regards analysis and as regards problems of policy. But, as regards the conduct of day-to-day affairs, the trouble is that in a world in which many different tendencies are developing simultaneously, it may not be easy to distinguish between the different types of influence on the balance of payments—the influence which is simply a reflection of changes in the real conditions of international supply and demand, including capital movements, and which serves the purpose of international equilibration, and the influence which arises from inflation abroad and which has no equilibrating function whatever. It would not be difficult to cull from the history of the last twenty years conspicuous examples of just such perplexities. How much, for instance, of the spectacular flow of funds into Germany has been due to the splendid economic performance of the people of that country, and how much has been due to inflation in the world outside, conspicuously the United States and the United Kingdom?

But now let us concentrate on the movements which are inflationary whether they occur first in one country, or group of countries, or in the world as a whole.

First as to causes. As regards the proximate influences—the causes which actually trigger off the excess expenditure as distinct from the ultimate conditions which make them possible or allow them to continue—I see no reason at all to deny their multiple nature. Ultra-cheap money—ultra-cheap, that is to say, in relation to profit prospects; government expenditure in excess of revenue; trade-union pressure for wage increases out of line with productivity; undervalued rates of exchange—you can find excellent examples of all these influences in the history of Western countries since the war. All such can be regarded as influences initiating the excess of aggregate expenditure over the value of the local product at constant prices which is the common characteristic of all inflations. There is no reason to believe on this plane of analysis that there is only one process of causation operating everywhere. It would be a waste of time to elaborate this point with detailed case histories.

But now I am going to say a very philistine thing: if we dig deeper, we can unearth an absolutely common characteristic—the failure of the financial authorities to bring it about that the excess of aggregate expenditure does not arise. This is obvious enough in all those cases which can be grouped under the heading of demand inflation: the excess of expenditure arises there directly because of the absence of adequate curbs. In the case of cost inflation, it is true that the pressure for increased incomes is not initiated by governments; the piteous shrieks and exhortations emanating from such quarters are surely evidence which, on that plane, we need not be concerned to deny. But it is also true that, if the money were not forthcoming to finance the results of such demands, there would be a fairly speedy upper limit to the effectiveness of this pressure. It is possible, though not frightfully plausible, to conceive of increases in the velocity of circulation which might sustain the movement for a short time, even though the money supply were expanding no more rapidly than real productivity. But I cannot believe that this could happen for very long. It is therefore clear to me that, in the last analysis, it is the failure to restrain the sources of increased expenditure which, in cost inflation as in demand inflation, is ultimately responsible for the trouble.

So in the end, whether they realize it or not—and some of them are pathetically unaware of it at the present time—it is governments which must bear the blame for what happens. It is their failure to control aggregate expenditure which is the governing condition that allows inflation to arise. Surely, we should all agree that the ultimate control of aggregate expenditure is a matter which, under modern credit systems, is inescapably the function of government and can be left to no other agents in the economic system.

I put the indictment this way—failure to control aggregate expenditure—rather than in the narrower way in which it is sometimes put—failure to control the increase of money—because I am anxious to leave no doubt of the eclecticism of my approach. I yield to no one in recognition of the importance of control of the money supply; and I think our debt to those who have revived

emphasis on this factor, at one time almost unmentionable, can
scarcely be exaggerated. But I remain eclectic in this respect. I
am not prepared to pass a self-denying ordinance as regards the use
of the fiscal instrument. I agree that, in modern democracies, it
sometimes seems almost hopeless to expect that it will be wisely
used. But I can easily conceive positions in Utopia in which its
use, in conjunction with appropriate monetary policy, is likely
to inflict less strain on the economy than monetary policy alone.
And for that reason as well as a certain, perhaps disingenuous,
intention to deal gently with those who develop psychoses at the
mere mention of monetary policy, I use the broader formulation.
I naturally reserve the right to ask them at some later stage to
explain to me in words of one syllable a fiscal policy which can
hope to succeed with a complete absence of control of the credit
base.

But, cautious and conciliatory though I am anxious to be, there
is one very general and highly provocative observation which I
think must be made in this connection. It is that all the great and
injurious inflations so far in the history of the world have taken
place on a paper rather than a metallic base for the credit system.
Surely, this is obvious enough if one looks at the history books—
the assignats, the post-World War I mark and franc inflations
were not on a metallic basis. And the same is true of what is taking
place today, which, with the fall in the value of money since 1945,
has certainly assumed the character of one of the major historic
inflations. If anyone thinks that, despite the shop window, the
present currency systems of the world, with all their special pro-
hibitions and inhibitions and agreements regarding gold reserves,
conform in any sense to what one would expect of metallic systems, then I submit he should have his head examined. And I submit that we must admit that, with all its obvious inconveniences
and occasional mild inflations, metal has behaved better than
paper—at any rate, as regards inflation.

Having said this, I am sure that many of you will at once imagine
the appearance of a cloven hoof if my shoes were to be removed.
"Now we see what he's up to. He's asking us to go back to gold,"
you may say. I assure you that you are quite mistaken. I'm sorry,
Monsieur Rueff, I don't think we can go back to gold. And I do
share the hope that at some time in the future we shall succeed in

doing better. All that I want to do at this stage is to point out the incontestable fact that, hitherto, systems based on the random accidents of geological discovery and chemical technique have not done so badly as regards inflation as the present arrangements of so-called conscious control which claim to have transcended them. It is a fact which should be conducive to humility.

What then can be done? I confess I bring you no message of comfort, certainly not in terms of institutions.

Clearly, there is not a great deal that can be done by the International Monetary Fund to restrain inflation on a world scale. I have no doubt whatever that the sensible advice offered by Fund officials to particular communities on balance-of-payments difficulties may have done something to induce greater moderation in financial policies. I think, for instance, of the suggestion made to the United Kingdom chancellor after the devaluation of 1967 that if he paid some attention to control of the credit base, the outlook would not be quite so miserable. The suggestion was not inappropriate and, when observed, showed the result which one would have expected. But, apart from such modest functions, it is difficult to see what the IMF in its present position can do to prevent inflation in general. The IMF, and still more the Keynes Clearing Union—the U.K. suggestion for postwar monetary reorganization—were conceived essentially as means of mobilizing more credit than would otherwise have been available in order to prevent *deflation*. And the introduction of special drawing rights—in itself another splendid manifestation of supranational cooperation—was conceived in the same frame of mind. I certainly would not blame this great organization for what has happened since its inception. But no one who has seen, as I have, the representatives of potential debtor nations slavering at the mouth, as it were, for additional quotas and drawing rights, can believe that the existence of the IMF has been any great restraining influence on tendencies for aggregate expenditure to be excessive– at any rate, before the excess has taken place.

I need hardly say that if the Fund could be transformed into a genuine central bank for its members, with power to act on the total credit base of the Western world and to require special deposits for sterilization in circumstances when undue credit expansion was taking place in the world as a whole, the situation would be transformed, and we should be well on the way, for the nontotalitarian world at least, to something like a federal economic union. But while I can conceive such mergers on a smaller scale—there is a genuine urge in that direction in Western Europe at the present day—I confess I am not at all sanguine, for our generation or the next, of something so ambitious for the entire clientele of the Fund. I really do not see national finance ministries willing to surrender their sovereign rights to manage, or mismanage, their own monetary systems unless there has been a much closer approach to political union than seems at all likely on this cosmopolitan scale for many years to come. Moreover, let us remind ourselves that even if we had the framework of a federal reserve system for the Western world, the system would not necessarily work in a noninflationary way, if the will to work it thus were lacking. If I can say so without any sense of discourtesy to my hosts, we can see before our eyes at this moment that a properly organized Federal Reserve System in the United States of America hasn't sufficed to prevent a pretty brisk rate of inflation in the last few years. The machinery may be present, but if the intention to use it is not there, the inflation will probably go on.

Much more practical and down-to-earth than these conjectural visions of supranational cooperation is the question of what can be done by individual national communities which have the desire to opt out of this process.

Well, it is clear enough that they need not inflate if they genuinely wish not to do so. As the inflationary funds from abroad move in, they can be sterilized by being added to reserves, and up to a point this is not without its advantages. Strong reserves are not a bad thing in this uncertain world in spite of the existence of the IMF and the bankers' club at Basel. But if there are agreements not to draw gold from the centers with depreciating standards, then the indefinite accumulation of dollars or pounds, or whatever currency is involved, becomes a great nuisance and a very uncertain asset, having regard to the possibility that eventually the exchange rate of the currency concerned must crack. Moreover, the loss of

interest on funds which are truly sterilized is a cumulative burden—
a stiff price to pay for avoiding the consequences of other peoples'
imprudence.

In such circumstances, in my judgment, the eventual policy to
adopt is appreciation of the rate of exchange in some form or
other; and although I abate nothing of my disbelief in floating
rates all-round as a permanent solution of the world's monetary
problems, yet in circumstances such as those at present under
discussion, when the tendency of the float would be upward, I
see far less objection to resort to this device than I do in circumstances when the tendency is in the other direction and an encouragement to the government concerned to let the rate take the
strain and otherwise do nothing. Certainly, if I were adviser to a
government which was determined in some way or other to avoid
the importation of inflation, this is the policy which I would urge
them to consider, once their reserves were large enough.

But let me make myself crystal clear: I would urge it in the
interest of the prudent country concerned. I would not urge it
in order to get the inflating countries out of their difficulties. In
the days in which the present international monetary arrangements
were under discussion, we used to hear a great deal about the
iniquity of the policies of great powers which, by practicing positive deflation, sucked into their coffers the gold and foreign exchange of communities manfully endeavoring to maintain a
volume of aggregate demand calculated to maintain brisk employment at reasonable wage levels. And it was of course in this
context that the appearance of the scarce-currency clause in the
statutes of the International Monetary Fund was hailed with such
rapturous satisfaction by all of us immediately concerned. But
since that time, no currency has ever become scarce from the
practice of positive deflation anywhere; and we did not discuss
at all what has become the practical problem, in which countries
maintaining good levels of employment have been inundated
with gold and foreign exchange because of the financial laxity
of their neighbors. There was a fundamental asymmetry in our use
of pejorative adjectives; and, in recent years, I have found few
things more conducive to pure cynicism than the spectacle of the
inhabitants of areas of relative inflation reproaching the authorities

of the more prudent areas for their failure to appreciate their rates of exchange and so to save the political bacon of those who were really responsible for the trouble. This is a mixed conference; I therefore mention no names. But I dare say that one or two of you may guess what I have in mind.

Doubtless there are other expedients of a more or less ad hoc nature which will come under discussion in the course of our deliberations. But I must not attempt to cover too much ground or too much detail. I would not conclude, however, before returning to the more general considerations from which I started.

All the trouble which we are to discuss, all the injustice and distortion, both of orderly investment and of orderly international relations, springs in the end from a state of mind—a sort of collective schizophrenia on the part both of those who rule over us and those who are ruled. Nearly all of us condemn rising prices; nearly all of us are against inflation. Notwithstanding a few professional utterances to the contrary, it is still a dirty word in public discussions. But at the same time, too many of us are against the policies which would prevent inflation: fiscal prudence, a money supply not rising more than the growth of the gross national product, interest rates not artificially depressed below the point which reflects realistic expectations of the behavior of the price level. We will the end—the termination of inflation. But we are not willing to will the means.

Now I am sure that some of you will say, " This is too easy a way to depict our frame of mind. We're much more sophisticated. We all know what you've been saying. But what is the alternative? Widespread unemployment. And, called upon to choose, we regard the latter as the greater evil. "

I confess I regard this as unnecessary defeatism. I do regard unemployment as a very great evil. I am quite sure that, at earlier periods, some economists—I regret to say, myself among them—were remiss during the 1930s in not supporting measures which would have greatly mitigated the unemployment arising from positive deflation: for reasons of faulty analysis, we were not sufficiently alive to the duty of government to prevent or repair collapses of aggregate demand. But unemployment due to inadequacy of expenditure to support a reasonable use of capacity at constant prices is one thing;

unemployment due to demands on production which cannot be supplied at constant prices is quite another thing. And while if I were adviser to a government which was confronted with strong inflation actually in process, I should not advocate any final application of the brakes all at once—that would probably produce situations of widespread disaster—I would not hesitate to proclaim as the goal of policy the maintenance of expenditure not beyond the level of brisk employment with constant prices. And I should not have any inhibition in telling the trade unions that in future they must choose whether or not to price themselves out of the market at a constant or only a slightly falling value of money.

I think there is all the difference in the world between the obligation of government to prevent collapses in demand at a constant or a slightly rising price level and an alleged obligation to finance demands which go beyond this and involve all the troubles we know so well. And I do not see why, even if the world does not listen to us at once, we should not continue to say so. For I am quite convinced of this: that whereas it is quite possible to live with small inflations for quite a long time, all experience shows that, in the long run, inflations of a greater order of magnitude are not only incompatible with orderly economic arrangements but also are incompatible with political democracy and the decency and the culture which go with it.

III. WORLD INFLATION: FACTUAL BACKGROUND

Fritz Machlup

Chairman THORP: Lord Robbins was very careful in his presentation to leave open the exclusive use of numbers for our next speaker, Fritz Machlup, whose assigned topic is "World Inflation: The Present Situation." I have told Professor Machlup that he cannot have the rest of the conference to cover this assignment, though the topic might well warrant that much time. But Fritz is eminently capable of compressing an immense amount of information into the mini-period of time I shall make available. He has suggested that if there are points in his presentation that are not clear, he would be willing to be interrupted by what he calls "clarifying questions"; if there are points which are likely to lead to argument, he would prefer that they come later.

FRITZ MACHLUP: Let me say first of all that I shall not confine myself to numbers; I shall use the English language to the extent to which I am capable.

When I began studying economics at the University of Vienna, immediately after the First World War, we were having a rapid increase of prices in Austria and, when asked what the cause was, we said it was inflation! By inflation we meant the increase in that thing which many now are afraid to mention—the quantity of money. A German economist—I think it was Spiethoff—tried to find a German equivalent for the word inflation (he wanted to have everything Germanized), and he came up with the word *Geldblähe*, which in English means " money-swell." The reference was clearly to the quantity of money. Later, we became a bit more sophisticated, and said that inflation was an increase in effective demand or in aggregate spending relative to the supply of goods.

Well, it really does not matter what we call inflation if only we always remember to say what is being inflated—the quantity of money, or total spending, or effective demand, or incomes, or profits, or wages. Like our egos, these variables are all capable of being inflated. Thus, if we use the word inflation, there should always be a qualifying adjective. In my remarks this morning, when I speak of inflation, I shall either use a qualifying adjective or avoid using the word. After all, the word "increase" is just as good.

In any case, I would never have believed that anybody could publish a study on inflation, defined as rising prices, and at the same time completely omit any reference to monetary expansion. Yet we were treated a few months ago to just such a feat. In a volume published by the OECD [Organization for Economic Cooperation and Development], entitled *Inflation—the Present Problem*, there was not a word about money. There were masses of statistics and big hunks of tables, but not a single table of any kind on the stock of money. There were impressive econometric systems of equations, but money was not among the variables. Well, that's a strange thing. I can explain it only as an idiosyncratic perversion. I shall try to make up for this omission in my remarks this morning; I shall have much to say concerning money and the increases in stocks of money.

I was given my present assignment on very short notice, and therefore have confined my homework to ten important industrial countries. In alphabetical order, they are: Belgium, Canada, France, Germany, Italy, Japan, the Netherlands, Switzerland, the United Kingdom, and the United States. Beginning in reverse order with the United States, let us first take a look at the increase in the U.S. money supply. During the period 1953-64, the annual rate of increase was never as high as 4 percent, with the highest figure, 3.8 percent, occurring in 1964. Then in 1965, with the acceleration of the war in Indochina, the figure rose to 4.0 percent, in 1966 to 4.5 percent, in 1967 to 6.4 percent, and in 1968 to 7.4 percent. Quite a departure from the preceding period, as you can see. In 1969, the increase in the money supply fell abruptly to 3.8 percent, but in the first three quarters of 1970 had climbed back to an annual rate of 5.5 percent.

Of course, the United States is not the only industrial country in which the money supply has been increasing rapidly. For example, in 1968, when the money supply in the United States grew at the peak rate of 7.4 percent, the money supply in Japan grew by 14.2 percent, in Italy by 13.7 percent, in Switzerland by 11.2 percent, in Canada by 9.5 percent, in the Netherlands by 9.3 percent, in Germany by 8.4 percent, and in the United Kingdom by 7.1 percent. Only Belgium had what might be called a low rate of increase– 2.5 percent. And for the twenty-year period 1948–67, the United States had the lowest rate of money expansion of any of the ten countries in my list, averaging 2.4 percent a year, as compared with 13.1 percent for France, 12.7 percent for Italy, 10.2 percent for Germany (1949–67), 6.1 percent for Canada, and 4.6 percent for Belgium. The highest figure, interestingly enough, is for Japan, where the annual increase during the period 1955–67 averaged 16.5 percent. Another interesting case is France, where monetary expansion has been at a high rate until recently. After increasing at an annual rate of 19.0 percent in the very disturbed second quarter of 1968, the French money supply grew by only 2.0 percent in 1969 and by only 1.2 percent (annual rate) in the first three quarters of 1970.

In studying the mechanics of this monetary expansion, it is instructive to examine the balance sheets of the central monetary authorities. Mainly because of the persistent flow of dollars associated with the payments deficit of the United States, monetary authorities of other countries have in many cases experienced a massive increase in foreign assets. Annual increases of over 10 percent have been common in recent years, and in some instances the rate of increase has been much higher. In Germany, for example, official foreign assets increased at an annual rate of 98.5 percent in the second quarter of 1970, and at an annual rate of 151.7 percent in the third quarter of that year; and in Japan the growth rates in some recent quarters have been comparable. But these rates of increase have been very uneven, both from country to country and from year to year; and in the case of

France, a vigorous rate of increase throughout the earlier 1960s
was replaced by a decrease of 52.6 percent in 1968—the result,
of course, of the disturbances in May of that year.

However, monetary expansion in countries other than the
United States cannot be blamed entirely on an inflow of foreign
assets, since the domestic assets of central monetary authorities
have also been growing at a high rate—indeed, often at a higher
rate than foreign assets. Of the observed nine industrial countries,
other than the United States, only three—Belgium, Canada, and
the Netherlands—had a lower ratio of domestic to foreign assets
in 1970 than in 1963, and in some countries, including France,
Germany, Italy, and Japan, the growth in domestic assets was
much faster than the growth in foreign assets.

Let us now take a look at price statistics, beginning with consumer-price indexes. For the ten countries on my list, you probably
won't be surprised to learn that, for the period 1948-67, France
had the highest compounded annual rate of increase—5.7 percent.
But you may be surprised to learn that the United States shared
with Germany the distinction of having the lowest annual rate of
price increase, each country accounting for a figure of 1.7 percent
(the German figure excludes 1948, the year of the German currency
reform). In between, in descending order, are the Netherlands (3.9
percent), Japan (3.8 percent),[1] the United Kingdom (3.7 percent),
Italy (3.2 percent), Canada (2.3 percent), with Belgium and
Switzerland sharing a figure of 1.9 percent. In most of the ten
countries, the consumer-price level has been rising considerably
more sharply during the past four years than during the period
1948-67, and in the first three quarters of 1970 the annual rate
of increase was above 3 percent in all ten countries. The United
Kingdom led with an increase, at an annual rate, of 7.4 percent,
followed by Japan (7.1 percent), the United States and the Netherlands (both 5.8 percent), France (5.7 percent), Italy (5.0 percent),
Germany and Switzerland (both 4.1 percent), Belgium (3.7 percent),
and Canada (3.1 percent).

If we turn from consumer prices to wholesale prices, we find a
number of fine performances for the period 1948-67. Of the ten

[1] Japan figure for 1953-67.

countries, Italy and Japan had the lowest compounded annual
rate of increase (0.5 percent),[2] followed by Switzerland (0.6 percent),
with Belgium and the United States sharing third place at 1.0 percent
each. Only three countries had an annual rate of increase of over
2 percent: the Netherlands (2.6 percent), the United Kingdom (2.8
percent), and France (4.4 percent). Since 1966, with one exception,
the annual rate of price increase has been substantially higher than
for the period 1948–67. The exception is France, where the annual
increase—4.4 percent—was the same in both periods. The increase
in wholesale prices has tended to accelerate in most countries,
apparently reflecting international influences. In the first three
quarters of 1970, the highest increase, at an annual rate, was for
the United Kingdom (7.7 percent), followed by Germany (7.6 percent), France (6.9 percent), the Netherlands (6.2 percent), Italy
6.0 percent), Belgium (5.9 percent), the United States (3.5 percent),
Canada and Switzerland (both 3.1 percent), and Japan (2.6 percent).

Before leaving the subject of price trends, I would like to report
the results of an interesting experiment made by Ronald McKinnon.
Comparing three rapidly growing economies (Germany, Italy, and
Japan) with three slowly growing economies (Canada, the United
Kingdom, and the United States), Professor McKinnon discovered
that in the former group, the consumer-price index has tended to
rise much more sharply than either the wholesale-price index or
the export-price index, whereas in the latter group, the divergence
has been much less marked. Thus, on a 1953 base, the Japanese
consumer-price index in the first quarter of 1970 stood at 197.3,
the wholesale-price index at 114.1, and the export-price index at
only 94.8. That is to say, during this period consumer prices almost doubled, whereas export prices actually fell! The Italian case
is only slightly less spectacular. Again, the export-price level actually declined, while the consumer-price level rose by about two-
thirds and the wholesale-price level rose by about one-fourth.

In the slowly growing economies, the picture is very different.
In the United States, for example, the consumer-price index in the
first quarter of 1970, on a 1953 base, was 141.4, the wholesale-price
index was 125.3, and the export-price index was 129.6. Not only
did the export-price index rise more than the wholesale-price

[2]Japan figure for 1953–67.

index, but the spread in the rates of increase for the three indexes
was much less than in the fast-growing economies.

I shall now return to monetary statistics—in particular, to
statistics on the spectacular growth of Eurodollars and other Eurocurrencies. From the end of 1964 to the end of 1969, Eurodollar
deposits rose from $9.7 billion to $46.1 billion; if we include all
Eurocurrencies, the increase was from $12.2 billion to $56.2 billion. The increase in Eurodollar deposit liabilities has been
particularly dramatic since 1967; during the year 1968, they grew
by 48 percent, and during 1969 they grew by 71 percent!

This development deserves attention, not only because of its
magnitude and its rapid growth, but also because Eurocurrencies
are what I call "stateless money." Eurocurrency deposits have a
high degree of "moneyness," since they are considered as perfectly liquid, and they are "stateless" in the following sense.
Assume that a firm in Argentina holds a dollar deposit in London.
This dollar deposit is not counted in the money supply of Argentina,
because it is in dollars and in London; it is not counted in the money
supply of the United States, because it is in London, not in New
York; and it is not counted in the money supply of the United
Kingdom, because it is in dollars and not in sterling. So we have here
a stock of money which is stateless in the sense that it is not
included in the money-supply statistics of any country in the world.
I think you will agree that $56 billion is not a small stock and that
an annual increase of 71 percent is not a negligible increase. Anyone
who thinks about the rate of expansion in the world money stock
must not fail to take account of the increase in these Eurocurrencies.

In a moment, I shall reveal a bit of Eurodollar magic, but only
after we take a look at the gross reserves of the national monetary
authorities—that is to say, the sum of monetary gold, official
holdings of foreign exchange, IMF reserve positions, and (recently)
special drawing rights. The first thing to note is that world monetary
reserves increased very modestly in the years 1966 through 1969;
the compounded annual rate of increase was only 2.5 percent.
An alarming increase occurred in 1970, when world reserves
increased from $77.7 billion to $95.2 billion (including $3.4 bil-
lion in SDRs)—an increase of 22.5 percent.

The dollar component of world reserves increased only from
$15.8 billion at the end of 1965 to $16.0 billion at the end of 1969,

with some intervening ups and downs. If the large increase in
1970 had been spread evenly over the five-year period, it would,
of course, have been far less alarming. But now I must reveal that
the spectacular increase in official dollar reserves in 1970 was to a
considerable extent a matter of what we might call magic. I am
not referring here to the repayment of the large Eurodollar
borrowings by American banks, involving a huge *transfer* of dollars
from private hands via the foreign-exchange market to the central
monetary authorities; this is readily understandable. The magic
which I shall now expose involves the *creation* of official dollar
holdings via the Eurodollar market.

Let us assume that, because of the payments deficit of the United
States, the German central bank has been acquiring dollars, which, of
course, are dollars held in New York. Let us assume further that the
German central bank does not want to have its money supply
inflated; so it offsets the externally induced monetary expansion by
reducing its domestic loans. In this situation. . .

GOTTFRIED HABERLER: One question—is the inflow of dollars on
current or capital account? Or does it matter?

MACHLUP :   It does not matter. Now the board members of the
German central bank want to be very smart, and they say, "Interest
rates in the Eurodollar market are most attractive. But let's not
place our dollars in London, because Dr. Emminger doesn't like that;
let's place them in the Bank for International Settlements—that's
perfectly sound!" What happens then is that dollars are shifted to
the BIS's dollar account in New York. But the BIS is not satisfied
with interest rates obtainable in New York, and therefore places
the dollars in the Eurodollar market in London. London, of
course, does not wish to hold these dollars in New York—that
would be poor business; it wants to use them for Eurodollar loans
to those who are willing to pay a high rate of interest. Who are
these willing borrowers? Well, here are some Germans whose credit
has just been restricted by the German central bank and who are
therefore eager to borrow money. Where can they borrow it? In
London, of course. So here come the Germans, whose credit was
restricted in Germany, borrowing in the Eurodollar market in
London. But the Germans do not need dollars; they need D-marks, so
they offer their dollars to the foreign-exchange market in exchange
for D-marks, and from the foreign-exchange market the dollars go

to the German central bank, which has to buy them at the support
rate for dollars. With this addition to its stock of dollars, the German
central bank is able to repeat the process I have just described, by
placing them with the BIS.

You may call this a merry-go-round or you may call it a round
trip; in any case, what happens is that the German central bank, by
placing its dollars with the BIS, receives these dollars back from
German firms that borrowed them in London, and the central
bank will have two dollars for every dollar so placed. Please note
that the dollar holdings of the German central bank are now twice
the size of the amount acquired originally as a surplus in the German
balance of payments; placing dollars with the BIS eventually
doubles them, and this process could theoretically go on indefinitely.
If the German central bank were to continue its policy of offsetting, it could multiply its dollar holdings by any amount.

Sir ERIC ROLL: At what point in the circle does this doubling of
dollars take place?

MACHLUP: At the end of the round trip, which can be repeated
again and again. Originally, the German central bank has dollars in
New York; then it transfers these to the BIS, and afterwards, as a
result of the transactions I have described, it has to buy them back
to keep the dollar exchange rate from going below the floor; thus
it again has dollars in New York. This situation becomes statistically
visible in the monthly figures of the IMF publication, *International
Financial Statistics*. As of the end of 1970, the total foreign-
exchange holdings of central monetary authorities are recorded
as $43.8 billion. But total official U.S. dollar liabilities are listed
as only $24.0 billion and total official sterling liabilities as $6.6
billion. There is thus a discrepancy of $13.2 billion, of which
probably not more than $2.5 billion consists of official holdings
of other currencies, such as D-marks, French francs, and Swiss
francs. A large part of the $13 billion is simply the placement of
dollars by central banks and other monetary authorities in the
Eurodollar market—either directly or through the Bank for International Settlements.

Now the ridiculous thing is that, while the central banks are
riding on this magic merry-go-round, they complain about the
inflow of dollars, not realizing that it is their own dollars that
are coming back. This point is worthy of note, because a part of

what they call "imported inflation" may be nothing more than
the delayed effect of the operations of the complaining
central banks.

ROLL: Although I can't pretend to be an expert, I know a little
about the lending activities that go on in London, and German
borrowers are not particularly noteworthy by their presence. There
are a lot of other borrowers; I do not know what difference that
makes to the argument.

The next point I wonder about is Fritz's statement that the
German central bank restricts loans and that this is what makes
potential German borrowers go to the Eurodollar market in London.
But, in fact, is it not the case that what the German central bank, and in
doing is simply *not increasing* the availability of credit? It is not
actually restricting; it is simply not permitting the increase in credit
that would be possible on the basis of the inflow of dollar reserves.
Now this is a very different proposition from saying that there is
a restriction of credit availability. Perhaps Fritz would like to
comment on that.

MACHLUP: The answer to the second question is very simple.
During some weeks, the German central bank actually restricts. I
read the weekly announcement of the German central bank, and in
recent weeks domestic assets have actually been reduced. But in
any case, the central bank has restricted the supply of credit relative
to a very heavy demand for credit, and this sends the would-be
borrowers to foreign markets.

Now, with regard to the first question, I have no policeman telling
me who appears in the London Eurodollar market. I have no inside
information concerning the extent to which Germans are actually
there in person or the extent to which the borrowing may be done
by others. My conclusions do not depend on such information.[3]

ROLL: I can see that.

LEONARD S. SILK: I have two questions for clarification. My
first question concerns the increase in dollar holdings of the German
central bank. Isn't this related, after all, to American price movements
and to changes in interest rates? My second question has to do

---

[3] In a note to the editor in 1972, Professor Machlup writes: "The suspected fact of
large borrowings by German firms in the London market has subsequently been confirmed."

with the Bank for International Settlements. Why does it place its
dollar holdings in London? Is it for the interest advantage simply?

MACHLUP: That is correct; in order for the BIS to pay high
rates of interest, it has to earn high rates of interest; so, naturally,
it places dollars where it receives the highest rates.

SILK: Right, but what about my first question on the relationship of American policies to the dollar holdings of European central
banks?

MACHLUP: Do you mean the original inflows of dollars?

SILK: Yes.

MACHLUP: Of course I would agree that American policies
have affected the American balance of payments, leading to a continuous excess supply of dollars abroad, in the sense that present
exchange rates can be maintained only by central banks purchasing
the dollars which the private sector does not wish to hold.

SILK: But that effect could be quite delayed; in other words, we
might have been quite wicked in 1967 or 1968 and very virtuous
in 1969 and 1970, but the punishment might come long after the
crime.

Chairman THORP: This begins to be argumentative, though
Gilbert and Sullivan are always appropriate. However, we have to
move ahead. Bob Mundell has something to say.

ROBERT A. MUNDELL: I was wondering if I might make a brief
point here. There is an immediate direct market effect of this
neutralization operation which comes from the very first attempt
on the part of the German central bank to sterilize. Interest rates
go up, and more capital comes directly into Germany. I would
add that, while the German central bank is big enough to conduct
such a policy, the Netherlands central bank, for example, certainly
could not do so effectively, because it is too small to affect the
capital market significantly. But my main point is that the effects
we are talking about don't have to proceed through all these
channels; they can be direct and immediate.

MACHLUP: I agree fully, but I do not believe that these sterilization attempts are really successful in the long run.

GIOVANNI MAGNIFICO: In this connection, it should be pointed
out that if a central bank is accumulating claims on the rest of the
world, and wants to prevent that accumulation from affecting—at

least to the full extent—the reserve position of the commercial banks, then it must actually reduce its claims on the domestic sector.

MACHLUP: Yes, right; that is what Emminger has really tried to do. Indeed, Emminger recently said that the fact that Germany has attracted all these dollars has probably reduced the rate of monetary expansion all over the world, because if the same dollar flow had gone to other central banks, there would not have been as vigorous an effort to sterilize it. But Emminger apparently did not realize that the effect of dollar placements with the BIS has further swelled the flood of dollars into Germany.

JOHN EXTER: Fritz, are you arguing that this process which you have described is different in kind from the process that occurred in 1959, 1960, and 1961, when Germany also attracted dollars and was forced to appreciate the D-mark? Is this a difference in kind or is it simply a mechanical difference?

MACHLUP: Well, I do not know what a difference in kind is if you say that a mechanical difference is not a real difference. The difference in the two situations is this: in both cases, the high rates of interest attract foreign funds, but in the present case, it is not merely new funds that are attracted; Germany *re-attracts* the funds which Germany, itself, has placed in the market. This is a big difference—a difference in kind, if you like.

EXTER: But wasn't that also true in 1960 and 1961?

MACHLUP: It was not; what happened then was merely a high rate of interest which, by attracting foreign funds, made the offsetting attempt futile. But in 1960-61, the German central bank did not, as far as I know, place any of its dollar holdings with the BIS; and there was not the active Eurodollar market at that time.

Chairman THORP: I shall let Mr. Fleming ask the last question, so that Fritz can finish his presentation.

J. MARCUS FLEMING: Regarding Mr. Exter's point, wouldn't it have been better if Fritz had started this whole chain, not with the influx of reserves into Germany, or with the sterilization, but with the German central bank's decision to shift from holding dollars in New York to holding dollars with the BIS?

MACHLUP: Yes, I agree, that is the key consideration.

Let me now return to the main stream of my remarks. Originally, I had intended to devote considerable time to cost-push and demand-pull inflation, but Lord Robbins has given us such an excellent exposition of these matters that I can greatly abbreviate what I have to say.

My main point is that the cost-push element in price inflation is now much more credible than it used to be. There was a time when economists were inclined to say that cost-push was merely a response to demand-pull. People like Milton Friedman would have said, "Well, the trade unions would never have obtained the high wage increases if there had not been a willingness to create the money that would support the higher prices made necessary by the wage boosts." This view is now far less widely held. The fact that several countries have experienced strong cost-push pressures despite large unemployment has convinced most of us that there is something to cost-push inflation, even if it remains true that such inflation could not persist if we were prepared to accept the massive unemployment that would ensue in the absence of a monetary expansion sufficient to support the increase in the price level.

Let me conclude with a few remarks about the problems of international adjustment created by the recent increase in national money stocks, in stateless money, and in commodity prices. My first point concerns the direct price adjustments of tradable goods at fixed exchange rates. If there is an increase in the United States in the prices of tradable goods, there will be—even without any monetary expansion elsewhere—an immediate parallel increase in the prices of these goods in all countries that maintain fixed exchange rates, simply because of the normal arbitrage mechanism. This mechanism, of course, involves a flow of money from countries in which the price increases originate to other countries, leading to demand-pull in the latter countries. As Lord Robbins showed, the process may be accompanied by imbalances in international payments and by maladjustments in exchange rates—effects which may occur both when only one country is the villain and when some countries are inflating more rapidly than others.

International adjustment in these cases can take place either through an adjustment in exchange rates or through acceleration of monetary expansion in the countries that have been inflating least. This leads me to my final point, which is on the subject of currency appreciation. Currency appreciation by the surplus countries is indicated, but not in order to benefit the countries that have inflated more rapidly than others; on the contrary, appreciation of the currencies of surplus countries bottles up the demand inflation in the immoderate countries, and prevents the latter from getting the goods and services which they would otherwise have received from the countries with the more modest expansions of demand. So the idea that Germany or Japan should appreciate their currencies "for the benefit of the rest of the world" is simply ridiculous; as long as they resist appreciation, they continue to supply the rest of the world with goods and services they would otherwise have for themselves. If the countries with a taste for greater price stability were to adjust their exchange rates upward, they would avoid needless price inflation, and would help to balance international accounts—an endeavor which, as Lord Robbins pointed out, should be pursued in *their* interest, even if it makes life more difficult for the rest of the world.

IV. THE ISSUES: FIVE VIEWS

Gottfried Haberler
Sir Roy Harrod
Robert A. Mundell
Jacques Rueff
Robert Triffin

Chairman THORP: During the noon break, the chairman held a damp finger in the air, and found that winds were blowing vigorously as a result of Fritz Machlup's statement this morning. While it might seem appropriate to talk about that now, I shall avoid opening Pandora's box at this point, as I might not be able to get it closed before the end of the afternoon. Instead, I propose to open, shall we say, Machlup's Eurodollar box tomorrow morning, when we can have a general discussion on the relation to world inflation of the large volume of stateless money in the form of Eurocurrencies. So instead of proceeding now with this specific topic, I suggest that we get added background from the five distinguished authorities who have joined me here at the head table. We shall begin with a statement by Gottfried Haberler.

GOTTFRIED HABERLER: We have had two first-rate speeches. We were told that we should go back to first principles, and the two speakers did exactly that. I agree with almost all Lord Robbins said, and I found Professor Machlup's remarks very intriguing. Let me comment on a few points which have perhaps not been stressed as much as I would have done.

Let me first say something about Lord Robbins's distinction between anticipated and nonanticipated inflation. This is a most important distinction. It disposes, in a way, of the Phillips curve—which no one has yet mentioned—which gives the "trade-off" between inflation and unemployment. The main objection to the

Phillips curve is that it leaves out the distinction between anticipated
and nonanticipated inflation. We are told very often now in the
United States that it would take, say, 8 percent unemployment to
get zero inflation. But that would clearly be much too high a price
for stopping the rise in prices; we would rather accept, say, 4 percent inflation in order to reach full employment. However, this
would not be a stable state of affairs, because people would expect
the price rise to continue. Interest rates would go up to compensate
for the expected inflation, and labor unions would press for larger
money-wage increases. That could be interpreted as an upward shift
of the Phillips curve. But I do think that the theory of the Phillips
curve has to be greatly modified to take the expectation factor
into account. This is one of the issues we might discuss later on.

Another controversial issue not directly related to international
aspects is the question of incomes policy. While not mentioning
the subject specifically, Lord Robbins had a number of things to say
which bear on this matter, and I think his present position reflects
some modification in his earlier views. One problem is that incomes
policy now means different things to different people. At this
point, let me just mention this as one of the fundamental issues in
the United States and elsewhere which we might discuss later.

I now turn to the international aspects of inflation. Let me begin
by making a very sweeping proposition, which obviously has to be
qualified somewhat but which I believe roughly applies—namely,
that the rate of world inflation is approximately determined by
the inflation in the United States. Expressed so boldly, this proposition will not be generally accepted, but let me say in what
sense I mean it.

First, let me make the obvious point that any country is free to
inflate more rapidly than the United States if it wants to. Many of
the less developed countries inflate more rapidly than the United
States and, as a consequence, they have to depreciate sooner or
later in open or disguised form. So my proposition applies only
to those countries which peg to the dollar—primarily to the industrial countries. For the industrial countries, by and large, I think
it is true that they have to follow American inflation unless they
change their exchange rates.

What are the exceptions to the rule? There is one exception
which I would regard as a spurious exception; a country can stave

off appreciating or depreciating, whatever the situation may be,
by introducing controls. But this is not a real exception, because
if a country introduces controls, it merely substitutes a messy kind
of partial depreciation or appreciation for a clear-cut change in the
exchange rate. So I would not regard this as an exception to the
rule. A real exception to the rule is that some countries manage to
have a little more inflation, or even substantially more inflation,
than the United States while at the same time having a favorable
balance of payments. Japan is an excellent example. In Japan, export prices have risen much less than the general price level, whereas
in the United States the opposite has been true. If you have such a
situation, then the country which enjoys a favorable export-price
performance can inflate more than the United States and still have
over-all balance, or even a surplus, in its balance of payments, as in
the Japanese case.

But the difference obviously cannot be very large. Under modern
conditions, there are hundreds of actual and potential export and
import commodities. For that reason, divergent price movements
are kept to modest dimensions. The difference cannot be as much,
say, as 6 or 7 percent per year in the price movement. So I think
we are not dealing with a really serious exception to, but rather
with a minor qualification of, the rule that countries which peg
to the dollar have to go along with the American inflation.

Another exception which should not be overestimated is that a
country can, for a time, sterilize the dollars which it receives if
it is a surplus country, or sell off part of its international reserves
if it is a deficit country. On the deficit side, of course, the reserve
loss is limited by the amount of reserves or the credit line available
to the deficit country; on the surplus side, a country can accumulate
as many dollars as it wants, but if the country really has a basic
surplus, and sterilizes, then the surplus is going to become unmanageable. Sooner or later, the country will have to appreciate
or to inflate.

But now let me explain why I say that there is this causation
from American inflation to the rest of the world. This, of course,
is what many Europeans say—that the United States exports inflation. While they are quite right in the sense that, so long as they
peg to the dollar, they have to have approximately the same rate
of inflation, what they overlook is that most countries, with very

few exceptions, quite spontaneously have had more inflation than the United States.

Lord Robbins has already commented quite correctly that if a country has the same degree of inflation as, or even a little more inflation than, the United States, as measured by wholesale prices or the cost of living, it does not follow that the country has generated that inflation spontaneously. The inflation may have been imported. In some cases, it is difficult to determine whether the inflation is imported or spontaneous; but I would suggest that a country which has to depreciate from time to time and in between maintains exchange controls—France would be a good example—is suffering from spontaneous rather than imported inflation. This is a matter which would require careful analysis, country by country.

Over most of the postwar years, most countries have managed to have more inflation than the United States. In the last few years, the situation has been a little different, but let me stress once more that this matter requires careful analysis. It is not sufficient just to look at the rate of increase in the cost of living or in wholesale prices; you have to go deeper, and I have indicated some of the points that have to be taken into account.

Why is it, then, that I say that other countries have to have as much inflation as the United States? Why do I not put it the other way around—that the United States has to have as much inflation as other countries? I state the matter as I do, because we are confronted with an asymmetrical situation. The reason is that the dollar occupies a central position. The dollar is the international reserve currency, the international intervention currency, and the principal "vehicle" currency. It is used for official and private purposes all over the world. The central position of the dollar is one factor which accounts for the asymmetry, and the other factor is that internal American policies which determine the rate of inflation are largely independent of the balance of payments. That, of course, was not so fifteen or even ten years ago; at that time, the United States had a large payments deficit, and internal policies were to some extent adjusted. Today, the discipline of the balance of payments is practically gone, and no government, Republican or Democrat, could afford to allow much more unemployment, or even a little more unemployment, on balance-of-payments grounds.

This is the actual situation. It is what I rather rashly called, in a little pamphlet, the policy of "benign neglect." I have referred to this now as a fact. I am quite sure that the officials will deny it, though I was careful in my pamphlet to say that benign neglect does not mean a neglect of American interest. It means that internal policies with respect to the management of over-all demand and with respect to the amount of unemployment which is permitted are determined by domestic considerations and not by the balance of payments.

Let me make one final point. There is, of course, a mechanical connection between the balance of payments and the domestic situation. A deficit has quite rightly been said to have a deflationary effect. A country which can run a large deficit can relieve its domestic inflation by importing more from abroad. That has a deflationary effect which is the counterpart of the inflationary effect on the surplus countries. But as far as the United States is concerned, the deflationary effect of the deficit is negligible, because imports are a small fraction of the gross national product. The deficit is an even smaller fraction—less than 1 percent of the GNP— so that, for the United States, the deflationary effect can be ignored. It could become important only indirectly: if it induced the monetary authorities to adopt an anti-inflationary policy.

I may have overstepped my time, but . . .

Chairman THORP: No, you have spoken for exactly the right length of time; thank you very much. Our next speaker is Sir Roy Harrod.

Sir ROY HARROD: I would first like to pay a tribute to our friend, Lionel Robbins. His marvelous oration, one might call it, was one of the finest expositions I have ever heard. I think we all appreciated it. My own pleasure from it began to decline in the latter part, because I found myself differing in opinion. In the earlier part, I was hopeful of agreement, because Lionel did distinguish between demand-pull and cost-push inflation. But in the last third of his remarks, this distinction seemed to me to become a little blurred in the phrase "excessive expenditure," and there seemed to be an implication that monetary and fiscal policies could have prevented this excessive expenditure.

Well, I don't believe they could have. We could have had more deflation in monetary and fiscal policies, but I don't agree with the implication that U.K. inflation has been due to laxity on the part of the authorities. I would say that in the United Kingdom there has been hardly any laxity on the money side. I've been over the figures, and for the last decade the increase in money supply has been only about 1 percent over the increase in real income, and 2 or 3 percent below the increase in money income.

That seems to me pretty conservative. You may say that there were certain months last year in which the money supply was allowed to increase more rapidly; but, by and large, the United Kingdom has pursued a very conservative money-supply policy. And it has had a terrifically deflationary fiscal policy; we've run these gigantic budget surpluses. Of course, the exact size of the budget surpluses is a matter of statistical interpretation, but on any interpretation the fiscal policy has been highly deflationary. It was never intended, when some of our industries were nationalized, that their capital requirements would all come out of the taxpayers' pockets, as they have been, with something over to reduce the national debt.

There may have been some slight aberration in monetary policy, but only for a few months. The wage-price explosion that has been occurring in the last eighteen months is altogether out of proportion; it seems to me that you have no instinct for figures if you say that this wage-price explosion is the effect of some slight deviation of monetary and fiscal policies from the perfect level.

But what is the cause of the wage-price explosion? I don't think it is economic. If you go back for a decade, you see similar aberrations on the side of monetary and fiscal policy not followed by wage-price increases of anything like the same magnitude. This new wage-price explosion is altogether unprecedented, and my own opinion is that the causes are sociological. The causes of our present difficulties are first cousins to the causes of such things as student unrest. We are dealing with a sort of activism on the part of people who want something for themselves—the labor unions, if you like, but also the corporations saying, "We'll just make our customers pay." All of this has been made possible, of course, by a certain permissiveness. Instead of employers presenting a stern front and saying, "We can't possibly give you the wage increase you want," they have been permissive. And the consumers have been permissive too; they just take the prices asked for in the shops, and don't argue about them as they would have in the old days.

So I think the problem is sociological rather than economic. Well, if that is so, you and I have to think again. This is a new phenomenon, and we've got to have a new policy to cope with it. We must cope with it, because I wholeheartedly agree with everything that Lionel has said about the evils of inflation. But I think we need another weapon which I don't think he mentioned at all in his oration—namely, incomes policy. Lionel offers instead an old idea: tell the wage-earners that if they go on making excessive demands, they will get fewer jobs. Well, when will they get fewer jobs? Because if the government has a policy of restricting demand whenever there is a rise in wages regarded as excessive, it can create unemployment whenever it wants to. Does Lionel mean that? This seems to me an awfully back-handed way of dealing with wage-earners and labor unions that demand too much. Why not simply say, "You can't do it." I would say that we've got to have an incomes policy as a necessary extra weapon in this postwar world where we regard it as a primary object of policy both to prevent inflation and to maintain full employment.

My second point will be shorter. This is something that I thought of before coming here, and is partly the result of my reading, for review in the *Economic Journal*, the papers of another conference—the "Bürgenstock Papers." These papers, as you all know, are concerned with the subject of flexible exchange rates. This is a subject on which I have been torn during my life as an economist—at times inclined to greater flexibility, at times doubtful. I agree with Lord Robbins that there does seem to be a tendency, under greater flexibility, to have more devaluation than appreciation. If that is so, a greater flexibility would have an inflationary impact on the world economy. There is another point; if you have a devaluation, you can't prevent it from having some inflationary effect, whereas the upward valuations don't seem to have much deflationary effect in the countries which appreciate.

Chairman THORP: Thank you very much, Sir Roy. I am sure
that your specific points will be discussed later. The next speaker
is Robert Mundell.

ROBERT A. MUNDELL: I shall follow an example of Milton
Friedman, and be precise in establishing disagreement. I am in
about 99 percent agreement with Lord Robbins, about 80 percent
with Professor Machlup, about 40 percent with Professor Haberler,
and about 10 percent with Sir Roy Harrod.

Chairman THORP: If you are running a declining table, it is
going to be tough on Rueff and Triffin when you get to them!

MUNDELL: There are just two little points on which I disagreed
with Lord Robbins. The first concerns the International Monetary
Fund. I think the IMF can do much more than it has; it may not
be able to stop inflation, but it could do a great deal toward
correcting it. My second point is about the cost of inflation. I
agree that if everybody anticipated it, no harm would be done, provided inflation came about in a particular way. Now that appears
to establish a disagreement. Actually, Lord Robbins was quite
careful in establishing that the increase in money came about
through changing the unit of account; money-holders are then
compensated immediately, and the adding of zeros amounts to
paying interest on real money balances. Optimal properties thus
are retained.

Professor Machlup's talk, almost uncharacteristically, had a great
many facts, but I don't think that he helped us to identify the
purely theoretical origins of inflation. As to Professor Haberler, I
do not believe that the United States should neglect the balance
of payments, whether the neglect is benign or malignant. If you
accept the opening of his argument, that we are on a dollar standard,
then the U.S. payments deficit becomes a means by which the
United States feeds the rest of the world with dollar reserves; and
to say that we should neglect it is to say that we shouldn't be concerned with the rate of reserve expansion in the rest of the world.

The reason that I am in so much disagreement with Sir Roy
Harrod is that he attributes inflation to nonmonetary causes. If
inflation is the price of goods in terms of money, then certainly
the quantity of money is an important aspect of it. The rise and
fall in the value of money cannot have a nonmonetary cause in
any significant sense of the term unless we are playing with semantics.

Looking at the basic causes of inflation, I have jotted down four types of inflation that I think have been historically important. One is a kind of structural inflation in which certain prices rise. You can have an inflation that is induced just by a harvest failure. I agree with Lord Robbins that we should not regard a price rise thus caused in anything like the same way we regard a price rise caused by an increase in the money supply. Second, you could have an inflation like the one that occurred after the Black Death in 1349, when a third or more of the people of Europe died and the (hard) money stock stayed where it was. Prices went way up. Again, that's a different kind of inflation.

But a major structural inflation may have come, I think, in the decade of the 1960s, through a rise in the efficiency of the use of capital. I am thinking of technological innovations connected with the communications industry, which have increased the efficiency of organization and exchange. Now, suppose the natural rate of interest rises abruptly from, say, 4 percent to 6 percent. To make the adjustment, there must be a fall in the price of future goods relative to present goods. You can get that adjustment with constant present prices and falling expected future prices, or you can get it through keeping expected future prices constant and letting present prices rise. The latter element, in my judgment, has been a factor in the U.S. inflation of 1965–69, and reflects a higher return on capital. If one were to stabilize an intertemporal price index, present prices would rise and expected future prices would fall.

Cost inflation is a different kind of problem—a matter of the dog chasing its tail. Monetary expansion leads to rising prices, the rising prices lead to rising wages, the rising wages lead to unemployment, the central bank expands the quantity of money in order to reduce the unemployment, and the circle repeats itself. Cost inflation is important only when labor unions have a monopoly and employers lack alternatives. In ordinary times, Detroit workers cannot say, "Let's now have a 10, 15, or 20 percent yearly increase in wage rates"—and expect to get it. Of course, everybody wants higher wages, and the labor unions are very powerful, but they don't normally demand 15 or 20 percent increases in wage rates; they can get only a 3, 4, or 5 percent yearly increase in normal times, and they know that if they opt for too much, plants will move to another location in the short run, while in the long run there will be a substitution of machines for labor.

It is only where uncertainty reigns about the monetary standard in a situation of general inflation that you get extravagant wage claims. In the steel industry, a 35 percent wage increase was demanded over a three-year period. Part of that demand—perhaps a third or half of it—can be regarded as an inflation premium, either catching up with past price increases or anticipating future rises. But labor doesn't know now what to expect about inflation, so the unions that make long-term contracts simply strike out for as much as they can possibly get, in order not to fall too far behind. If we had a stable monetary environment, the demand would not, under any stretch of the imagination, be 35 percent; it would be more like 15 percent, which might still be too high but would be within reasonable relation to productivity growth.

This is where the monetary authorities are at fault. They have failed to preserve a "fair" monetary environment—and injured members of the public are bitter. Only in this sense is the sociological theory valid; but the initiating cause is monetary instability.

In what sense is this a world inflation? Are we dealing with a situation in which all countries are to blame, or is one country—the United States—the major villain? There is one school of thought which says that we can always find particular reasons for the inflation in France or in Italy or in Brazil, and that we don't have to blame the United States. Actually, the situation is rather complicated. If you look at the data examined by Professor Machlup, you see that, while the dispersion of the rates of monetary expansion among countries of the world is very great, the dispersion of the rates of price inflation is not very great. This is because, throughout the world, as David Hume knew, prices and inflation rates are connected, and cannot diverge much from one another. There is a single world price level now in which prices, broadly speaking, move together, even though weights in individual cost-of-living indexes are different. That world price level has been going up far more rapidly than ever before, and we are therefore justified in speaking of a *world* inflation.

I think that one fundamental explanation of this inflation has been the change in the world monetary standard. Indeed, we might call the phenomenon "monetary standard inflation." The dollar took over as the world standard some time in the 1960s. As a result, the base of the world monetary system is no longer gold but the dollar, and the expansive potential of the dollar has been tremendous. When an ordinary national currency is promoted to the position of a monetary "base," the inflation potential takes a quantum leap. The key to the expansion, of course, has been the U.S. payments deficit which, to an important extent, has been the reflection of U.S. inflation.

Now why does the United States inflate? It inflates because of the belief that unemployment will be minimized. And this brings me to the Phillips curve, mentioned by Professor Haberler. The economic cost of the Phillips curve theory has been enormous in the United States. I don't believe that the Phillips curve has ever really existed in the sense in which it has been used. Inflation does not reduce unemployment unless the wage-unit is constant, or at least rises less rapidly than prices.

There seems to be a widespread belief that an increase in the money supply will reduce unemployment, but that belief does not really arise from either classical or Keynesian theory. Keynes never argued that an increase in nominal money supply will correct unemployment; to achieve the latter aim, you have to increase the money supply *in terms of the wage-unit*. But that may be impossible in a world where wages are flexible. We have believed for a long time that wage rates are rigid downward, but no one has ever presented any evidence that wage rates are rigid upward. Actually, of course, wage rates are highly flexible upward, so that the effect of increasing the money supply may not be a larger money supply in terms of the wage-unit but, rather, a change in expectations about inflation that leads to an increase in money-wage rates. Clearly, an increase in the money supply of 10 percent, accompanied by a 15 percent increase in wage rates, would cause a decrease in employment under classical theory, under Keynesian theory, or under any theory at all. So monetary expansion does not correct unemployment; what it can do, of course, is to offset the effect of wage increases on real wages.

The implications of all this are very serious. In 1968 our problem was to stop the inflation without causing a depression. How should we have done that? Should we have done it through monetary policy or through fiscal policy? The actual policy was a tax

surcharge—a move that reduced effective demand and thus was
partly responsible for the recession that came about in 1969-70.
After the tax increase, the inflation actually accelerated. This
should not really surprise anyone, since, with a given rate of monetary expansion, a tax increase should lower output expansion and
thus increase prices. And when inflation occurs in a progressive
tax system, the budgetary policy becomes even more stringent
than intended, because people move into higher tax brackets. By
any calculation of budgetary tightness, there was great stringency
in 1968, 1969, 1970, up to the present time. I can only conclude
that the administration's answer to the question of how to stop inflation without causing a depression was the wrong answer, because
the policy adopted caused a depression without stopping inflation.
By any calculation, the cost of the recession is between $90 billion
and $150 billion. And the inflation certainly isn't over yet.

What, then, is the appropriate policy? My first observation
would be that monetary and fiscal policies do not have the same
effects on the economy. Monetary expansion has an effect upon
expectations that is different from fiscal expansion. Fiscal
expansion has a bigger effect on the real variables in the economy,
and monetary policy has a bigger effect on the rate of change of
the value of money, the reciprocal of the inflation rate. The right
policy, I think, is to split monetary and fiscal policies, using
monetary restraint to check inflation, and tax reduction—which
would reduce the upward wage pressure—to increase employment.

Let me summarize. Part of the problem of world inflation is
correctible and part of it is not, because I think there has been
a rise in the real full-employment rate of interest—and, to reflect
that situation, we need some increase in present prices relative
to future prices. For the United States, the cure for the correctible part of the inflation lies in monetary restraint combined
with a budget deficit to mitigate the unemployment—which, at
6 percent, is a tremendous cost to the United States and to the
world economy.

Chairman THORP: Thank you, Bob. We next turn to Jacques
Rueff.

JACQUES RUEFF: I greatly regret my uneasiness in the English
language, because I feel that what we have heard today requires a
great deal of discussion, and I am afraid that I shall be unable
to express matters as I see them.

Among the most important topics already discussed is this extraordinary expansion of Eurodollar currency. Let me say first of all that I have never thought that an expansion of currency is a primary cause of inflation; I am convinced that it is an effect, not a cause. In the years just before World War II, one might argue that I was the man responsible for inflation in France, because I was in charge of the treasury. Yet I never decided any issue of currency; every Wednesday evening, the central bank sent me the account of the treasury in the central bank, which simply reflected the expenditure of the treasury, and the money was issued without any order by anybody. The currency issue was the result of aggregate expenditure, and the amount of currency, as I said, was a result, not a cause. If I were to discuss this matter with my friend, Milton Friedman, I would express much doubt about the causal effect of the issue of money, and would say that the amount of currency issued simply reflects the desires (as transmitted through various channels) of money-users for cash balances. These needs and desires impose on the central bank the creation or destruction of money.

I now come to the very important and illuminating speech of Lord Robbins this morning. He looked at me when he spoke of gold. There may be some misunderstanding about my position on this matter, but there is none about his position, because he said quite clearly that he doesn't think we can go back to gold. I know that whenever Lord Robbins speaks, he has very good reasons for his views, and I am sure that he has some other solution in mind. I suppose that what he has in mind—he will deny it if I am wrong—is some kind of administration of the monetary regime based on special drawing rights. Am I wrong?

Lord ROBBINS: I haven't any clear conception of the system's future. In my speech, I was concerned with the fact that the supply of gold is no longer the effective regulator of the volume of credit. That seems to me to have been true for quite a long time, and the simple point that I was making was that probably we have passed the point of no return. I am not optimistic about the immediate future. I simply ventured to draw attention to the fact that, in the past, gold systems have behaved better than the systems that have been superimposed since, and to express the hope that, sooner or later, we might improve upon this rather dismal record.

RUEFF: I have been indiscreet in asking you this question, but I am glad to have more precision on the matter. Lord Robbins says that gold is no longer a regulator of the issue of currency. I agree. But let us see what kinds of regulators exist and what are the results. We cannot do without a regulator; we must have one, and I suppose that we would all agree that the regulating function is now exercised by the central banks of the world.

Let us look at the results in recent years. Consider the situation in the United States. Let me say that my remarks are made with all possible respect for the U.S. monetary authorities, who are in my view the most learned in the world. But that being said, let me point out that in July 1965 the secretary of the treasury declared in print that the deficit in the U.S. balance of payments would be reduced by half at the end of 1965 and would entirely disappear by the end of 1966. I need not tell you that this prediction was not borne out by history. Another example: At a conference in 1967, the ministers of finance of Germany, the United States, France, Italy, and the United Kingdom declared that they had decided to cooperate in order to reduce interest rates in their countries. Well, the rate of interest on long-term loans in the United States at that time was 4½ percent; at the end of 1970, it was 6 percent, and you know that it was even higher after that. Finally, in July 1967, the Group of Ten decided on the creation of a new reserve instrument which would make possible the orderly expansion of international liquidity required to meet the needs of trade. This was done on the assumption that it would be impossible in the future to count on further increases in official holdings of dollars as reserves. You all know what has happened. Last year, more than $3 billion was created in special drawing rights—in a year during which official dollar reserves increased by about $9 billion—and another $3 billion in SDRs has been created this year, in spite of the continued expansion of dollar reserves.

I dared in 1961 to formulate a diagnosis of the world monetary situation. I must say that I was nearly alone. I say "nearly," because my good friend, Robert Triffin, agreed with me on the diagnosis, though not on the remedy. My diagnosis was that this extraordinary regime in which we were living—the gold-exchange standard—could not avoid having three consequences: first, the perpetuation of the U.S. payments deficit as long as the gold-exchange standard continued; second, inflation in the creditor countries as long as the U.S. payments deficit continued—and as long as the official dollar receipts were not converted into gold; and third, the eventual collapse of the system in view of the increasing "credibility gap" caused by the continued accumulation of dollar claims on an amount of gold—U.S. gold—which was not increasing, but decreasing.

Well, I am sorry to say that this diagnosis has been abundantly verified during the past decade. As to my first prediction, the deficit in the U.S. balance of payments has persisted, and last year was at a record level. As to my second prediction, we are in the gravest inflationary crisis in the world in many, many years—the inevitable result of the continuous purchasing by the surplus countries of the dollars required to finance the persistent deficit in the U.S. balance of payments. Finally, as to the collapse of the system, it has already happened; in March 1968 the system exploded, and was transformed into a pure dollar standard, with results that are exactly the same as those which have always occurred under inconvertible currencies.

What is to be done? I can only give my own conclusion that I do not see any practical, safe instrument in the present state of the art of central banking other than a gold foundation—not gold only, but gold with credit, as was intended in the Bretton Woods system. I have never proposed, as some people seem to think, a suppression of credit creation, but I consider gold as the ultimate means of settling international deficits. Whatever its deficiencies, such a system is far less dangerous than the one we have today.

Chairman THORP: Thank you very much, Mr. Rueff. I think we have to say that you have made a direct contribution to the conference by deflating the central bankers. We now move on to Bob Triffin.

ROBERT TRIFFIN: I would like first of all to thank my learned friends for stealing my thunder; they have left very little for me to say. I will therefore say little, but I will try to look at the forest rather than the many trees that we have been looking at all day. At the risk of vast oversimplification, I will also try to be more precise as to the kind of remedy or solution that we should look for, even though central banks and governments may not yet be ready to accept it.

My first observation is that the international monetary system has long been in a process of gradual evolution, from bimetallism to the gold standard, from the gold standard to the gold-exchange standard, and from the gold-exchange standard to what we have today. In my view, the year 1970 marks an acceleration of that evolution into a revolutionary pace of change.

We can even speak of a double revolution. The first revolution is one that most of us would praise—the first creation of "paper gold." The purpose of this reform is to pave the way for a rational management of the world monetary system. I applaud this very much; I consider it a milestone for the future. But the future we are talking about still seems somewhat distant, because, in establishing this milestone, we did not do anything to clean up the past. We did not decide what role would be left for gold or for the reserve currencies in the new system, and the result is the second revolution, which I do not applaud. This is an unwanted revolution, in which the new paper gold has been totally swamped in 1970 by the paper dollar.

The first reaction of central bankers to these developments has been to question whether there is any justification for creating further SDRs. After all, special drawing rights were invented to prevent a shortage of world liquidity; if we have a flooding of world liquidity, should we still add to our SDRs? My comment on that is that, even if there had been no creation of SDRs last year or this year, the liquidity system would still have been flooded with dollars.

This brings me to some brief comments on the balance of payments of the United States. I would like to draw your attention to one extraordinary fact which, I think, has not been emphasized by economists. It is this, that while balance-of-payments figures for the United States and for other countries move up and down in puzzling gyrations, there is one item which remains extraordinarily stable. That is the export of U.S. capital, which has slowly risen from a level of about $9 billion a year in the early 1960s to a level of about $11 billion in the early 1970s. Nowhere in the balance of payments is there so much stability as in that figure. The same is true of the balance of payments of the United Kingdom, and for the same reason: that because of financial, economic, and political considerations, you cannot close the City of London, and you cannot close Wall Street. This is perhaps the most obvious fact of life in the balance of payments.

Since these exports of U.S. funds have been very much in excess of the U.S. current-account surplus, the difference of course has had to be covered by inflows of foreign funds into the United States or by losses of U.S. reserves. To take a quick look at recent developments, in 1968 Wall Street was booming, interest rates were high in the United States, and the U.S. balance of payments, according to both official definitions, was temporarily in surplus because of a large inflow of nonbank funds which were not counted as part of the deficit—and rightly so. In 1969 this inflow of nonbank funds was sharply reduced from $6.8 billion to $4.6 billion, and what happened? American firms borrowed $9.2 billion from commercial banks abroad. This created havoc with the balance of payments on a liquidity basis, transforming the surplus into a deficit, because the borrowings were counted as part of that deficit; but the United States remained in surplus on an official-reserve-transactions basis. Then in 1970, as Professor Machlup indicated, American firms began to repay some of the borrowings of the previous year. Under the rules of the International Monetary Fund, foreign monetary authorities had no choice; when the repayments tended to depress the dollar below 99 percent of parity (99¼ percent under the European Monetary Agreement), central banks were compelled to step in and buy dollars. Thus the United States had an official-reserve-transactions deficit that year of about $10 billion, a deficit without any precedent in the past.

I find it really remarkable that, in an international monetary system in which most central banks are under various kinds of legal or traditional restraints on the creation of domestic credits, no such restraints are placed on central bank lending to the United States. The sky is the limit. Of course, you may say that central banks can offset the inflationary impact of their accumulation of dollars by reducing domestic credits. But is this really feasible in the long run? Will governments and public opinion accept the fact that central banks will have to curtail domestic credit in order to accommodate—without any limit whatever—the financing of foreign policies in which they have no voice? To my mind, this is a completely unacceptable approach to international monetary problems if we look beyond a few years.

It is true, of course, that central banks have one or two other options. They can inflate, and let prices and costs catch up with prices and costs in the reserve-center countries. Well, this is clearly not an attractive solution either. Another option for surplus countries is to appreciate their currencies. The difficulty with this solution is that it imposes upon countries which are not to blame for the situation, the political onus of correcting the deficit of the United States; and this is very difficult in a world in which currencies are tied to the dollar. Moreover, in a situation where it is the dollar that is out of step, a country may understandably be reluctant to appreciate its currency unless other countries are prepared to do so too. The French, for instance, might be willing to face the fact that, with a more expensive franc, Citroën and Renault would be confronted with increased competition from Ford and General Motors; what they could not face would be increased competition, not only from Ford and General Motors, but from Fiat and Volkswagen. So the political problem is difficult, and is largely responsible, I think, for the renewed drive toward monetary integration in Europe.

Thus, while I agree with those here who feel that, in view of the present situation as it has developed, some exchange-rate adjustments will probably be necessary, I also agree with Lord Robbins in not systematically favoring this approach as the best way to run an international monetary system.

This brings me to a word about exchange-rate flexibility. We can advocate such flexibility until we are blue in the face, but as long as central banks are free to intervene in the market as they like, we cannot force that solution upon them. If there is one instrument which would force flexibility, it would be an agreed ceiling on the amount of foreign exchange which central banks could accumulate as part of their monetary reserves. That means really changing the whole engine. With the present engine, inflation is spread throughout the world, because central banks automatically accumulate dollars, thereby relieving the United States of any balance-of-payments discipline.

Let me end with a quotation. Long before President de Gaulle characterized the role of the reserve currency as an exorbitant privilege, the American colonies complained about taxation without representation. And at about the same time, somebody in Europe wrote the lines I would like to read to you. I find them extraordinarily perceptive.

> No objection can be taken to seeking assistance, either without or within the State, in behalf of the economic administration of the country, such as for the improvement of highways or in support of new colonies or in the establishment of resources against dearth and famine. A loan, whether raised externally or internally, as a source of aid in such cases is above suspicion. But a credit system, when used by the powers as a hostile, antagonistic instrument against each other, and when the debts under it go on increasing indefinitely and yet are always liquid for the present (because all the creditors are not expected to cash their claims at once), is a dangerous money power. This arrangement—the ingenious invention of a commercial people in this century—constitutes, in fact, a treasure for the carrying on of war; it may exceed the treasures of all the other States taken together, and it can only be exhausted by the forthcoming deficit of the exchequer—which, however, may be long delayed even by the animation of the national commerce and its expansionist impact upon production and profits. The facility given by this system for engaging in war, combined with the inclination of rulers toward it (an inclination which seems to be implanted in human nature), is, therefore, a great obstacle in the way of a perpetual peace. The prohibition of it must be laid down as a preliminary article in the conditions of such a peace, even more strongly on the further ground that the national bankruptcy, which it inevitably brings at last, would necessarily involve in the disaster many other States without any fault of their own; and this would damage unjustly these other States. And, consequently, the other States are justified in allying themselves against such a State and its pretensions.

For those of you who haven't guessed, the quotation is from Immanuel Kant's booklet, *Eternal Peace, a Philosophical Essay,* published in 1795.

V. DIALOGUE ON THE ISSUES

Members of the Conference

Immediately following the five statements recorded in the preceding chapter, members of the conference were given an opportunity to continue the discussion of issues relating to inflation as an international problem. This dialogue, which occupied the remainder of the first afternoon, is reproduced below.

R.H.

Chairman THORP: We are now ready for an open general discussion of issues relating to our conference theme. The first person who has asked for the floor is Sir Eric Roll.

Sir ERIC ROLL: I'd like to make a very brief intervention, which is partly inspired by the closing remarks of Robert Triffin—more particularly, by his quotation from Kant. This brought to my mind another quotation from the same work, which, if my memory serves me rightly, is something like this: "That philosophers should become kings, or that kings should philosophize, is hardly to be expected, nor is it to be desired; for the possession of power inevitably corrupts pure reason." Now until Robert spoke, I thought that we were going to have nothing but an appeal to pure reason today, but he has now introduced the political element into our discussion, and this seems to me to be very valuable. He introduced it at the international level.

Similarly, on the domestic level, when I heard Lionel Robbins this morning in his usual brilliant, comprehensive, and most appealing exposition of the whole problem, I couldn't help feeling right at the end—when he spoke about what he would have to do if he had to advise the government on what to do—that if I were a counselor of a king, I would find myself frustrated by the advice that he was giving me. Up to now, the only purely noneconomic reference which has been made to possible ways of combating inflation is the reference to incomes policy by Roy Harrod. I won't say what some people might expect me to say in this connection, "Sir, you are speaking of the woman I love." That is not the point, even though, in my previous incarnation, I had a brief affair with the lady. I don't mean that incomes policy is a panacea by any means, and I don't think Sir Roy meant that either. What I believe is that we may be faced in a country like Britain, for example, with a new phenomenon for which ordinary economic analysis, even at the sophisticated level evident here today, is not really adequate.

Our problem is a wage explosion. Of course, it may be that the wage explosion in Britain, as some maintain, is simply the somewhat slow result of sterling devaluation in 1967. But whatever its origin, it may be a development which, consciously or not, is deliberately designed to change the pattern of income distribution in the community. If that were so—I'm not saying it is—then obviously the ordinary means of economic policy—fiscal, monetary, and so on—could still be brought to bear on the situation with some effect, but not with sufficient impact to deal effectively with all aspects of the problem. I do suggest to you, Mr. Chairman— and this is where I will stop—that both in the international field and domestically, it is worth spending a few moments on the extra-economic aspects of the problem with which we are dealing.

Lord ROBBINS: May I just say one word, Mr. Chairman. When I referred to the possibility of advising government, I was referring simply and solely to the advice that I would give to the German government on how to stop inflation. When I passed on to the wider question, I deliberately left out the wages-policy question, although I have spoken about it elsewhere and will speak about it here later. I'm not necessarily in disagreement with Sir Eric at all.

Chairman THORP: On behalf of the rapporteur, I would like to thank the two members who have cited quotations for choosing an author on whom the copyright has expired. The next speaker is John Parke Young.

JOHN PARKE YOUNG: For over a decade now, the international monetary system has been under intensive study. Much has been said and written, numerous conferences have been held, hearings have been conducted by the Joint Economic Committee, and a large amount of attention has been given to the subject by the IMF, the OECD, the Group of Ten, and others. The problems have been explored and reexplored. Yet we still have unsolved problems and an unsatisfactory system. We move from crisis to crisis, and the threat of the big crisis hangs over our heads. It is time now for further official action.

Several significant improvements have been introduced, such as the two-tier gold arrangement, special drawing rights in the IMF, the development of central bank cooperation, and extensive credit arrangements among central banks. But more needs to be done; and that is what we are considering here.

One of the most difficult problems—made more difficult by in-flation—is that of adjustment. Matters of liquidity and confidence would more easily fall into place if there were a reasonable solution to the adjustment problem. The adjustment problem arises principally because the world has to conduct business through a number of na-tional currencies and because these currencies are subject to diver-gent influences—in particular, to differing rates of national inflation. This situation leads into the question of exchange rates and how best to keep rates close to a level which promotes adjustment.

Regardless of debates over exchange-rate flexibility and other options to promote adjustment, if we were able to develop an inter-national currency medium to replace the dollar—one which enjoyed confidence and widespread usage—this would contribute signifi-cantly to a solution of the adjustment problem and, I might add, of some of the political difficulties associated with the dollar stand-ard.

The reason is that if there were such an internationally accepted currency—a true gold substitute and anchor in which there was confidence—exchange-rate adjustments of national currencies to such a currency would be less disturbing as transactions among countries, and also within countries, became increasingly denomi-nated in this world currency. Transactions and accounts denomi-nated in this currency would be largely insulated from national currency devaluations. Business would tend to use this currency

in order to escape exchange-rate uncertainties. There would be
less incentive to switch into strong currencies, with disturbing
capital flows and speculation. Some domestic transactions would
also tend to be denominated in the international currency when
there was lack of confidence in the local currency.

Widespread use of the currency, both internally and externally,
would reduce the significance and repercussions of exchange-rate
adjustments. Rate adjustments would not be such world-shattering
events. Such a currency would thus encourage more frequent
rate adjustments, and thereby assist in the maintenance of a pattern
of exchange rates more conducive to equilibrium. By facilitating
rate adjustments and greater flexibility of rates, the currency
would reduce some of the difficulties stemming from varying rates
of inflation among different countries. Insofar as it replaced the
dollar, it would facilitate revaluation of the dollar if this became
necessary. By replacing sterling, it would also help meet some of
the objections of France to absorption of sterling into a European
currency system.

As we look ahead to a European currency and two major
currency blocs (assuming that sterling is included in the European
bloc), it is evident that exchange-rate adjustments between the
two blocs would be of considerable consequence, with widespread
ramifications. A needed adjustment—and the problem of who
adjusts to whom—would be confronted with so many difficulties
that adjustment might be long delayed. Development of an international currency to the point of extensive use, although it would
probably take considerable time, would simplify exchange-rate
adjustments between the two bloc currencies.

It is sometimes assumed that close cooperation in monetary and
fiscal policies can keep inflationary movements in harmony, and
thereby obviate the need for exchange-rate adjustments. This view
oversimplifies the causes of disequilibrium, and expects too much
from the effectiveness of cooperation. We are reminded of the
vogue of the purchasing-power-parity theory after the first World
War, when price-level relationships were supposed to determine
the appropriate exchange rate. We know that structural changes
can build up to a point where disequilibrium calls for an exchange-
rate adjustment, even though prices have moved in a parallel manner with those in other countries. Cooperation, though obviously

desirable, cannot guarantee exchange stability or solve the adjustment problem. Plans of the European Economic Community for steps toward monetary union involve the hope that cooperation in monetary and fiscal policies will prevent the need for exchange-rate adjustments during the transitional period. With an abundance of good luck, this hope may be warranted, but the continuation of pegged exchange rates among the EEC countries cannot be assured, as EEC planners are aware.

Regarding the establishment of an international currency to replace the dollar, the question comes down to whether such a currency is in the realm of practicability or, considering the political and other difficulties, is only something to be dreamed about for the distant future.

In the long evolution of money, we have experienced a number of major changes. If we focus upon the past hundred years, we have seen the world abandon silver and bimetallism; adopt a largely uncontrolled gold standard; turn more and more to credit money alongside of gold; introduce between the two World Wars an increasing amount, and now a large amount, of monetary management in the interest of full employment, growth, and economic stability; extend the gold-exchange standard—or, more accurately, the dollar-exchange standard—throughout most of the world; establish the International Monetary Fund; expand central bank cooperation; and, now, debate where we go from here. Most of us agree that our international monetary system is inadequate for the vast amount of world trade and interdependence among nations. The system is like a house that has been built by adding a room here and a room there as the need arises, without any general architectural plan.

Looking at the evolution of the system and its inadequacies today, it appears clear that major changes lie ahead. We are getting accustomed to drastic economic and social changes, and to the overthrow of entrenched ideas—mostly for the better. The international monetary system is not immune. Changes in the system have usually come belatedly and as a result of emergencies and economic distress. Have we not reached the stage where we can repair the roof before the rain comes, or must we wait for trouble? Are we waiting for the big crisis? In our efforts to deal with immediate problems and to bolster the system, we should not neglect more fundamental remedies. The International Mone-

tary Fund and the World Bank are examples of the wisdom of
bold innovation.

The theoretical and practical aspects of reform of the international monetary system have been thoroughly explored and reexplored. We have the constructive proposals of Robert Triffin,
Edward M. Bernstein, Fritz Machlup, and others. What is needed
now is to pull the strings together and develop a concrete official
proposal for submission to members of the IMF for action.

A workable and not unfamiliar plan to provide the world with
an effective international currency medium would be for the International Monetary Fund to open an account in terms of a new unit,
perhaps equal to the SDR, and establish transferable credits in this
account for fund members. The credits would be acquired by member countries through deposits of gold, SDRs, and convertible foreign exchange, and would constitute part of the participating
countries' monetary reserves. The unit could be defined in terms
of gold, but would not be redeemable in gold, although a partici-
pant withdrawing from the arrangement could receive back the
gold it had put in. Participation of Fund members in the plan should
be voluntary in order to expedite its establishment. The arrangement could start with a few members; countries would soon find
it in their interest to participate.

Commercial banks could maintain accounts in the IMF currency
at their central banks. The currency would be bought with local
currency by commercial banks from the central bank, which would
acquire it from the International Monetary Fund as needed and as
related to the country's balance-of-payments position and holdings
of gold, foreign exchange, and SDRs. Commercial banks could
make the funds available to private users, and the currency would
thus make its way into general use as demanded.

I would not minimize the difficulties, political and other, of
creating such a currency. But it is time to start moving from discussion to action. If certain measures are not possible today, we should
nevertheless take steps to help make them possible tomorrow. Such
a currency would not require establishment of a thorough-going
world central bank, for which the world is not yet ready; it is essentially the further development of SDRs.

In order to get on with the job, it would be well if the board of
governors of the IMF appointed a small committee of governors,
which would operate largely through deputies, to develop specific

proposals for further improvement of the international monetary system. The terms of reference of the committee should be broad. Instructions should include preparation of plans for a monetary unit to be available to central banks *and the public* as an international currency medium. This would be one of the committee's main tasks.

From the many proposals which have been made regarding the international monetary system, the committee would sort out, put into concrete form, and endeavor to obtain preliminary agreement on those proposals which it felt merited adoption and had a reasonable chance of acceptance. The committee would seek advice both from the Fund staff and from outside economists.

Such an assignment is a large order, but one from which we should not run away nor put off any longer. In view of the long time needed to plan, to resolve differences, to contend with endless debate, to prepare concrete recommendations, and to obtain final action, moves along the foregoing lines should not be delayed.

WILSON SCHMIDT: I would like to say a few words about the question of whether countries are importing inflation from the United States. In reviewing the literature, there seem to be at least four main channels for propagation.

The first is a kind of demonstration effect, where inflation in one country, such as the United States, leads to expectations of inflation in another, this all somehow being validated by changes in the velocity of money. But when one looks at the data presented by Professor Machlup on the behavior of prices in the United States as against other parts of the world, one hardly can suggest on these grounds that the United States is the source of inflation for the world as a whole, since U.S. inflation began later, and has been at a lower rate, than in many other countries.

A second line of argument in the literature is the cost-inflation approach, where it is argued that increases in import prices lead to increases in other prices, which lead in turn to increased wage demands, resulting in cost inflation. Again, if one accepts this hypothesis, the facts don't seem to support the notion that the United States is the source of worldwide inflation, since U.S. export prices have risen more slowly than price levels in many countries abroad.

The third sort of effect has been a liquidity effect which Professor Machlup has analyzed in terms of foreign assets and domestic assets. His data clearly show that domestic-asset expansion is a more important source of inflation than foreign-asset expansion.

Finally, there is the aggregate-demand explanation, which is focussed on what happens to the balance of payments in goods and services. In recent years, the U.S. surplus in goods and services has declined from its peak level in 1964 to a level about $7 billion lower. But if we compare this $7 billion with a gross national product for European OECD countries of almost $700 billion, it equals only about 1 percent of the total demand for goods and services in that area—hardly enough to explain the very large inflation that we perceive in Western Europe and elsewhere.

GIOVANNI MAGNIFICO: Let me expand briefly a point I made earlier. In maintaining a given volume of liquidity, central banks, depending on circumstances, may have to substitute the foreign component of their assets for the domestic component, and when the situation changes, to do the reverse. Now, underneath this monetary aspect, there is a real one—the fact that when a central bank has to reduce domestic assets in order to make room for foreign assets, what is taking place is an export of real resources. In a word, the community is making forced savings, and this process is bound to create inflationary tension, whether the central banks succeed or fail in reducing domestic assets.

Let me close by saying a word about Eurodollars.

Chairman THORP: I'm sorry to interrupt, but I am going to let you do that tomorrow morning when the Eurodollar market will be specifically under discussion. Next is Gardner Patterson.

GARDNER PATTERSON: I have been struck by the fact that the subject of this conference is world inflation; yet in a full day's discussion by a group of people whose names would dominate the bibliography of any important international economic subject, only one has had a word to say about the possible role of commercial policy in relation to this problem. That man was Professor Haberler, who, to my great surprise, implied that commercial policy probably would have only negligible effects.

But I wonder. It seems to me that in a period such as we are now going through, the fact that imports may be a fairly small percentage of GNP doesn't tell us very much. After all, imports operate on the margin, and to the extent that we have cost-push inflation now in so many countries, with pressure for wage increases far in excess of any increase in productivity, we may have a very potent weapon if we simply remove trade restrictions in strategic sectors. We have a steel problem coming up in the United States where very substantial wage increases appear likely. No one can doubt that these wage boosts will have an inflationary effect on the whole economy. But this is a matter in which we are not helpless. As I am sure you know, the United States restricts the importation of steel not just by tariffs but by so-called "voluntary" export restraints exercised by the Western European producers as well as by the Japanese. I can't help believing that if, as a matter of policy, these restraints were removed or reduced, we would have put into operation a very powerful anti-inflationary force.

I cite this as one example. I have been struck by the fact that two countries with a good record for financial prudence—namely, Switzerland and Canada—have recently speeded up a series of tariff cuts that had been planned to be spread over a longer period under the Kennedy Round negotiations; and they did it for the specific purpose of helping to control internal inflation. As a GATT official, I'll admit that I am not an unbiased observer on this question, but I would strongly counsel further consideration of this approach to the problem of world inflation.

ARTHUR I. BLOOMFIELD: I would like to make a brief comment on the policy of "benign neglect" of the U.S. balance of payments. Professor Haberler is, of course, quite correct in saying that the world is now on a dollar standard and that the dollar is, in effect, inconvertible into gold for substantial amounts. The United States is thus in a position to tell foreign monetary authorities that it is up to them to adjust by currency appreciation, by more expansionary monetary policies, or by import liberalization if they wish to avoid further unwanted accumulations of dollars. There is surely considerable logic in this position. Yet I believe that it would be unwise for the United States to remain altogether indifferent to our continuing payments deficits.

My view of this matter is based fundamentally on political considerations. Rightly or wrongly, the monetary authorities of the leading surplus countries are fed up with being presented with the choice of accumulating further dollars which they do not want or of taking adjusting measures themselves. They deeply resent what they consider to be the inequities associated with the privileged position of the dollar and the United States under present international monetary arrangements. They have complained bitterly over what they regard as the benign neglect that the United States has already displayed toward its payments deficits in recent years. For those of us who are Americans to disregard these grievances, legitimate or not, after promising for years to keep our deficits under better control, could further strain or embitter political relations with our friends abroad, to the possible detriment of our broader foreign-policy objectives and with possible adverse repercussions on our economy.

At the very least, I do not see how we can properly afford to disregard our role in promoting, or to be passive in the face of, the massive private short-term capital outflow from the United States during the past year, which had contributed heavily to the accelerated build-up of foreign official dollar reserves. Instead of relying relatively more on fiscal ease in our effort to lift the economy out of recession, we permitted a very sharp decline in short-term interest rates, to the obvious neglect of its balance-of-payments consequences. Meantime, European countries, lagging behind us in cyclical phase, in many cases were still keeping money tight in their fight against inflation. The resulting international gap that was opened up in short-term interest rates provoked large-scale movements of funds from the United States to Europe via the Eurodollar market, thereby flooding European central banks with further dollars. Domestic economic goals should, of course, have priority over the balance of payments, but the latter should not be entirely neglected in our choice of domestic policy mixes.

In the past few months, we have permitted some tightening in short-term interest rates, and we have undertaken special official borrowing operations in the Eurodollar market to mop up dollars that would otherwise flow into foreign official reserves. That we took such actions, however belatedly, suggests an awareness on our part that we could no longer wisely neglect the balance-of-payments consequences of our recent policies and the political implications of the greatly increased build-up in foreign dollar reserves. So long, at least, as present international monetary arrangements remain in place, we will probably have to continue to show a greater sensitivity to the external effects of our domestic policy mixes than we have in the recent past.

RANDALL HINSHAW: While we are on the subject of benign neglect, let me say that I learned from Arthur Bloomfield this noon that the expression can be traced back to Lord Norton, a

British official who, more than a century ago, advocated a policy of "benign neglect" for Great Britain in its relations with Canada. Lord Norton doubtless had the painful British experience with the American colonies in the back of his mind, and one wonders how the history of the world would have been affected if his advice had been followed in the 1770s.

Whatever its origin, the term is clearly a useful prescription in certain situations, but in applying it to the U.S. payments deficit, I think we should distinguish sharply between that part of the deficit which is caused by U.S. inflation and that part which might be called a necessary part of the so-called dollar standard. I have no doubt in my own mind that a large part of the U.S. deficit, particularly in recent years, has been caused by U.S. inflation. But as long as we have the present system, logic prevents me from wishing that removing the inflation would completely remove the deficit. Under present arrangements, I am quite sure that the world would be just as unhappy with U.S. external balance as with a moderate U.S. payments deficit, and would be even more unhappy with a persistent U.S. payments surplus. For the dollar standard implies a U.S. payments deficit in some degree, and it also implies at least some central bank cooperation by the rest of the world to make the system continue. Otherwise, I entirely agree with that great Frenchman, Jacques Rueff, that the system could not persist, and I also completely agree with him that the system contains no automatic adjustment mechanism.

Let me hastily add that I hold no brief for the present system. But it is the system we have, and we should accept its implications until we replace it, as some of us—including me—would like to do. The problem here, of course, is that we are not agreed on what we want to replace it with.

Let me also add that I most emphatically do not believe in benign neglect of the U.S. inflation. But if we are talking about the U.S. payments deficit, I greatly prefer benign neglect to what one might call malignant concern. For excessive concern about the deficit has led the United States to do, or threaten to do, some highly dubious things—and here I would include most of the measures that have been taken both in the field of capital transactions and in the field of current transactions. I refer especially to the very real threat of U.S. import restrictions, which I fear may

emerge not only because of protectionist pressures but because of
a resurgence of concern over the payments deficit. Earlier, Gardner
Patterson expressed surprise that no one except Professor Haberler
had yet raised the question of trade measures in relation to the problem of world inflation; I assured Gardner that this was partly because I had not yet had an opportunity to speak.

JACQUES RUEFF: Let me say a word about the dollar standard
and, more generally, about the gold-exchange standard. The United
States is not responsible for the dollar standard; the Americans
never asked for it. The creditor countries—though they did not
know what they were doing—are really responsible for the system,
because they include dollars as assets on their balance sheets, and
they issue money against these dollars. In this connection, I should
point out that, while central banks have never been forbidden to
have foreign exchange for their current needs, the Bank of France—
to cite the case I know the most about—was not entitled, except
for a brief period during the 1920s, to list foreign exchange on its
balance sheet until 1936, when the practice had become fashionable. So the gold-exchange standard—and, more particularly, the
dollar standard—is something rather new. Of course, Americans
have discovered the benefits they can draw from the system, but
they are not to be blamed for creating it; I want to make myself
quite clear on that point.

GORDON K. DOUGLASS: I would like to return to more general
matters by adding some thoughts on the causes of world inflation.
Numerous institutional changes have occurred in the international
economy since World War II which might have contributed to the
new inflation. Aggressive national growth policies, increased
unionization, the adjustable-peg system, and "stateless" money
have all probably played a part. Since each of these developments
already has been mentioned by other members, let me add multinationalism to the list.

By multinationalism I mean the internationalization of oligopo-
listic market behavior. This latest stage in the evolution of business organization has several important effects—in particular, a
new militancy in labor organizations, an aggravation of balance-
of-payments disequilibria, and an undermining of the power of
national authorities to implement effective expenditure and
"switching" policies. Although these effects do not wholly explain

why inflation has accelerated and has diffused so widely during the last three years, they do explain why—if multinationalism is left uncurbed—worldwide inflation may continue indefinitely.

Perhaps the most interesting of these effects is the role of multinationalism in the aggravation of payments disequilibria. Multinationals behave like their large national ancestors: they eschew price competition, and they favor the tools of product differentiation. On the one hand, this imparts a ratchet-like upward motion to prices as corporate policies—and union pressures—successfully press for higher prices and even more sucessfully resist lower ones. And on the other hand, the quest for new processes and new products, especially through large outlays on research and development, sets the stage for technological-gap trade and for the difficult adjustment problems—for both leading and lagging countries—which "new-goods trade" creates.

The disequilibria created by new-goods trade are more frequent and probably more intractable than those dealt with in traditional theories of trade and adjustment. This means that, as the volume of new-goods trade rises in proportion to total trade, adjustment mechanisms must work harder to restore payments equilibria. In the meantime, the inflationary biases of today's monetary systems take charge, feeding on what increasingly seem to be chronic deficits and surpluses.

How to curb this additional bias toward world inflation is a far from easy question to answer. More flexible exchange rates might help in some degree, but a trading world dominated by new goods with low price elasticities would not respond easily to switching devices. Better international control of cartels would help, but the prospect of international agreement seems remote. In short, the rising importance of multinationalism is adding yet another inflationary bias to the international economy—a bias which cannot easily be offset by actions of existing international institutions.

RICHARD BLACKHURST: I would like to raise the issue of whether there is any agreement here about what constitutes a "problem" rate of inflation. We have talked about inflation being serious, and we have data on individual countries, but we haven't defined when an inflation is moderate and when it becomes serious, nor have we said anything about what criteria we should consider in attempting to make such a distinction. Lord Robbins expressed dis-

may about a recent statement by Harry Johnson to the effect that
we should learn to live with inflation. A little later, he was telling
us about the bad effects of the German hyperinflation. Clearly,
he didn't mean to imply that Harry Johnson had said we should
learn to live with hyperinflation; yet the two statements were in
close conjunction. My point is that perhaps our discussions would
be more fruitful if we could agree on what constitutes a problem
rate of inflation. Behind this, of course, is the basic question of
what determines the optimum rate of inflation or, more generally,
the optimum rate of price change. This question predates the
Phillips curve controversy and, as far as I know, has never been
satisfactorily answered. It also encompasses a number of more specific questions. For example, is there any reason to believe that the
optimum rate of price change for one country would also be the
optimum rate for another country? And if the rates differed, what
implications would this have for the international monetary system
if countries were able to achieve their different optimum rates?

Chairman THORP: There will be no more speakers this afternoon. Tomorrow morning, we shall focus our attention on what
some might call the new elements in the world monetary picture.
In particular, we shall take a closer look at the spectacular growth
of the Eurodollar market and its relevance to the problem of global
inflation.

VI. EURODOLLARS: THE ROLE OF "STATELESS MONEY" IN WORLD INFLATION

Members of the Conference

A major mystery in the acceleration of inflationary tendencies since the mid-1960s has been the role of the rapidly growing Eurodollar market—a market which, as Professor Machlup had pointed out in his address, has thus far eluded both national and international supervision. Among the conference members were several leading authorities on the Eurocurrency market, and it was unanimously agreed that the conference should explore this highly technical and highly controversial subject. Accordingly, the second morning of the conference was entirely concerned with the role of Eurocurrencies in world inflation. The dialogue is recorded below.

R. H.

Chairman THORP: The time has come, the chairman says, to speak of many things. Yesterday, if anything was clear, it was that world inflation is a highly complex subject reflecting numerous forces—proximate, distant, economic, sociological, political. Today, our problem is how to handle ourselves in such a way as to produce the most thought from the largest number of people in the limited amount of time we have. I suggest that we devote this morning to this rather new notion of stateless money, as reflected in the Eurodollar market, and its relationship to world reserves and the general problem of inflation. I am asking Professor Swoboda, a distinguished Eurodollar expert, to open the discussion.

ALEXANDER SWOBODA: I shall not spend a great deal of time on this problem, partly because I don't think we know enough yet to devote a great deal of time to it. Let me try simply to state a few of the possible connections between the problem of world inflation and the Eurodollar market. I think one can distinguish at least three such connections.

The first connection between the world inflation problem and the Eurodollar market concerns the transmission mechanism. Here I would say that the Eurodollar market acts as any efficient international capital market would act, and it is not terribly important that it happens to be the Eurodollar market. The important thing is simply that we have an efficient international money market, in which interest-rate changes in one part of the world spread very quickly to the rest of the world. If one large part of the world, such as the United States, changes its monetary policy in any abrupt way, the change is going to be transmitted very rapidly through the international monetary mechanism to the rest of the world.

A second connection is the role of the Eurodollar market in frustrating attempts by individual countries to use monetary policy to affect aggregate demand. Here again, the issue is not that the Eurodollar market has greatly altered the picture, but that we have an international money market where flows of funds from one country to another tend to be very responsive to interest-rate changes and, as a consequence, are likely to interfere with national monetary decisions.

The third connection seems to me the most interesting—the connection between the Eurodollar market and what we might call the world money supply. If we believe that there is any connection between the quantity of money held by the public and the rate of inflation, and if we are talking about world inflation, then we should certainly be concerned with the quantity of money in the world. One way that we could define the world money supply would be as the sum of all money held by the public in the various countries. This would be the sum of the national money supplies plus some other things, like stateless money.

We can ask ourselves what the determinants of the world money supply are, and we can start with a very simple view of the world— let us say, a strict gold-standard view. In such a world, growth in the money supply can come from three sources. One source would be an increase in the domestic assets of the central bank; a second would be an increase in the quantity of international reserves (in this case gold); and a third would be a change in the banking system's customary or compulsory reserve ratio.

If we move to a more complicated system, such as the gold-exchange standard, then we are basically in the same situation, except that we now add one more source of possible expansion of the world money supply. In this situation, the reserves of central banks do not consist exclusively of gold but also include, say, dollars.

Now what happens if we decide to treat the Eurodollar deposits of individuals and corporations as money? Clearly, we have a further possibility for the creation of world money to the extent that deposits are created within the Eurodollar market without destroying liquidities elsewhere in the system.

As you know, there has been some controversy about multiplier effects in the Eurodollar market and about how important they may be. I think that if one performs any kind of reasonable hypothetical calculation, one comes to the conclusion that the multiplier which can be applied to any primary deposit in the Eurodollar market will be somewhere in the neighborhood of 1.5 or 2, but not much larger. In this connection, Professor Machlup yesterday opened Pandora's box with his Eurodollar illustration—a very significant illustration, because it suggests some additional possibilities for expansion of the world money supply. What his example suggests is that if central banks themselves place money in the Eurodollar market, and count that as part of their foreign-exchange reserves, then we get two things: first, we can incorporate that fact systematically into the so-called Eurodollar multiplier. For example, if central banks systematically redeposit half of their dollar holdings in the Eurodollar market, we would have to multiply the multiplier we have just talked about by two, giving a much more expansionary effect.

The other interesting possibility is that, to the extent that central banks count their Eurodollar deposits as reserves, the world monetary base is expanding in a way that no longer depends simply on the expansion of the domestic assets of the central banks or on the expansion of international reserves, whether gold or of the dollar kind. And one of the interesting implications is that these additional foreign-exchange reserves, which I understand Professor Machlup and Professor Triffin estimate to be somewhere around $10 billion, do not constitute a claim on the United States. They are just there; they are a claim on the private banking system but not on the United States.

I would like to develop a much more precise model of all this, but since I haven't done so, I won't say much more. But let me say just one word about the implications for world inflation. I don't think that we would want to say that, just because the possibility for multiple monetary expansion is greater now than before, world inflation is inevitable or is uncontrollable. It *is* controllable. Just because there are new financial intermediaries and slippages in the system does not mean that monetary policy is totally ineffective; it simply means that we have to push harder in order to get a given result.

Lord ROBBINS: I would like to ask Dr. Swoboda a question which kept rising in my mind as I listened to him and to Professor Machlup yesterday. I was brought up to believe that a stable credit system demanded a lender of last resort, and I should like to know where the lender of last resort is in the Eurodollar market—and whether the ambiguity of this situation is not one which really has quite substantial potential danger for the stability of the inter-national monetary system.

SWOBODA: It's a tall question; I'll try to give a short answer. I don't think that there is any single lender of last resort in the Euro-dollar market. The lenders of last resort remain the national mone-tary authorities. Of course, the most important national monetary authority in a sense is the Federal Reserve System, and in that sense it could be regarded as the lender of last resort in the Euro-dollar market. One analogy that Professor Machlup has used is the country-bank system in the United States, where you can get mon-ey creation at different rates in different parts of the banking sys-tem, although the lender of last resort remains the Federal Reserve System. In the Eurodollar market, we have the various national central banks. But, of course, the whole situation is terribly un-coordinated.

FRITZ MACHLUP: I might amplify the matter in this way. Lord Robbins was talking about the stability of the system, and I assume he was thinking of the possibility of severe trouble. I agree with him that the possibility of trouble is definitely with us and that we cannot count on the Federal Reserve System to bail out the Euro-peans if their credit pyramid should collapse. It will be up to the

European central banks to do that, and I do not see any indication that they will. Thus, I can imagine that a serious problem may arise.

Let me say one thing. In fine print, the Swiss banks have a provision according to which, should they be unable to collect their Eurodollar placements in other countries, they will not guarantee the safety of the dollar deposits of their own depositors. Of course, many of these depositors will say, "What could ever happen to the Schweizerische Kreditanstalt? It will pay its depositors!" Such people do not believe that the system can break down. But Lord Robbins has revealed a serious problem: there is no individual lender of last resort. We can perhaps hope that a consortium of European central banks would, in a crisis, get together to safeguard the Eurodollar obligations of commercial banks.

Sir ERIC ROLL: I am delighted that Lionel Robbins has raised this question; I was going to raise it had he not done so.

There is a source of potential trouble here which hasn't been at all appreciated yet. The development of the Eurodollar market has been very good for business, and, generally speaking, it has been very good for the London merchant banks. But there is no doubt that there is no genuine lender of last resort. The sources of funds that are being used by those banks that are going in for extending substantial medium-term credit in currencies other than their own national currencies—which means primarily dollars—are mainly either consortia-backed credit or standby credit of U.S. commercial banks. It is no good looking to the national central banks to provide the ultimate backing to this credit—even if it were theoretically feasible for them to get together—because the risk involved is the risk of the *nonavailability* of the currency in question; it isn't the credit risk, it is the risk of nonavailability. And the national reserves held by central banks—certainly as far as the Bank of England is concerned—would not be used, could not be used, and would not be adequate in the case of a really major confidence crisis.

Commercial banks of course differ in their practices, and there are some, without naming names, which are very, very careful in the extent to which they go into this medium-term credit business and in the extent to which they match their maturities, their liabilities, and their credit availment in this field. There are other banks which are not so careful, and there is undoubtedly a volume of uncovered positions that could—in the case, for example, of a major squeeze in the United States—cause very serious trouble.

ROBERT A. MUNDELL: I too want to emphasize that Lord Robbins has put his finger on one of the essential problems in world inflation—the lack of a lender of last resort (except, possibly, the Federal Reserve System of the United States).

There are two dimensions of this problem. One is the danger that the world money supply is explosive, and is no longer under the control of the monetary authorities of the world. Now, of course, ultimately the base of the system will be high-powered reserve money in the United States, but we have moved into a system where what is ordinary money in the United States—bank money, low-powered money, so to speak—becomes essentially high-powered money in Europe, so that ordinary deposits in Chase Manhattan Bank or First National City Bank in the United States form not only part of the money supply in that country, but also the base of a potentially explosive money supply in Europe. We have moved into a system in which the supply of money is almost completely determined by the demand for money, because there are always means by which clever bankers can find ways of turning ordinary deposits in the United States into the base for a much larger monetary expansion in Europe. This means that, at present, there is no effective means of controlling the world money supply.

The second danger is that the United States will clamp down at some point as world inflation builds up, and that we will get a succession of periods, as in 1966 and in 1969, where interest rates rapidly rise to 10, 12, 13 percent in a squeeze that ends in widespread bankruptcy. This is what Jacques Rueff was concerned about in 1960 when he asked whether the West was risking a credit collapse. The mechanism is somewhat different now, but the lesson is still the same. What must impress all of us is the fantastic growth in one decade of foreign-money deposits from a level of $3–$4 billion in 1960 to $60 billion or more today. This development was not planned, and is entirely outside the control of the world monetary authorities. It is an alarming situation. There is an element of uncertainty and ignorance about the system that should make us extremely concerned.

GOTTFRIED HABERLER: I should like to go back to first principles. When we speak of the Eurodollar market, we should keep in mind that we are talking about "real" dollars and not about

phantom dollars which are less usable than real dollars. The Eurodollar market is the consequence of American interest-rate and
capital-export controls. There is Regulation Q, which places a ceiling on the interest rates which American banks can pay on dollar
deposits, and there are the American capital-export restrictions.
If it were not for these two forms of restriction, there would be no
Eurodollar market. There would be a dollar market, of course, but
it would be more concentrated in New York. European banks
would participate in that dollar market along with American
banks, and I think it is quite useful to think our problems through
on the assumption that the partly separate Eurodollar market did
not exist. I believe that the growth of the Eurodollar market com-
plicates the analysis unnecessarily; the market is simply a way of
getting around the American controls.

Right now, as you have read, American banks have repaid their
loans in the Eurodollar market, because interest rates in the United
States are lower than in Europe. The year before, it was the other
way around. I think this is simply the consequence of the fixed exchange-rate system. If you have fixed exchange rates and convertibility, and if the cyclical phases in different countries diverge, of
course you get these capital flows, which go through the Eurodollar
market rather than through the general dollar market because of the
American restrictions. There is really nothing mysterious about it,
and I believe that it is misleading to speak of a special money-
creating function of the Eurodollar market. The lender of last
resort in a real sense is the Federal Reserve; there is nobody else.

So the whole huge growth of, and movement through, the Eurodollar market are the consequences of the fixed exchange-rate system, convertibility, and divergent cyclical movements. I have just
read a description in the last *Federal Reserve Bulletin* of what
happened in the Eurodollar market last year. It shows quite explicitly how these capital flows came about. You could cross out
the Eurodollar market completely; it is an intermediate market—
a sieve through which funds flow with a certain resistance, but fortunately the resistance is not very strong.

MUNDELL: But it is not right to attribute the whole Eurodollar
market to Regulation Q. If you abolished Regulation Q in the United
States, Gottfried, you would *not* abolish the Eurodollar market.

Chairman THORP: Let's hear Eric Roll on this. Eric?

ROLL: I just want to add a footnote. By the way, I entirely agree with what Bob has just said regarding Regulation Q. I want to add another point, because Gottfried also mentioned the capital-export controls in the United States. We have been talking about the short end of the Eurodollar market, but of course another very striking phenomenon as part of this whole development in the last eight years has been the long end—the Eurobond market—which has been perhaps even better for business, particularly for the City of London, than the money market.

The increase here has been fantastic. I think the first Eurobond issue was in 1963—appropriately enough, for the *autostrada* here in Italy—and since 1963 the total has reached something of the order of $16–$17 billion in long-term issues, primarily denominated in dollars, though there have been some in D-marks. This development I think can genuinely be ascribed, in large part at least, to the American capital controls—the interest-equalization tax and the ceilings on American bank lending abroad, at first voluntary, later mandatory, which have shifted the market to Europe. But I think we will agree that there is a tremendous difference between, for example, the development of capital exports from Germany in D-marks at a time of substantial balance-of-payments surplus and the development of Eurodollar bond issues at a time of record-breaking balance-of-payments deficit in the United States. What this situation demonstrates is the futility of trying to remedy a payments deficit by capital-export controls while maintaining the basic conditions which make the deficit continue.

Chairman THORP: We have two other bankers who have not yet had an opportunity to get into this discussion. The first is Mr. Magnifico.

GIOVANNI MAGNIFICO: I have one remark about the lender of last resort, not as regards the credit risk, but as regards the liquidity position of the market. I believe that all monetary authorities are lenders of last resort, the European central banks as well as the Federal Reserve System, because they all participate as lenders in the market. I would add that this fact has been noted by others; in the 1969 report of the Bank for International Settlements, I quote: "On various occasions, the banks obtained resources from central banks with a view to intervention on the Eurocurrency market so as to moderate the movement of funds on that market."

This explains in part why the Bank for International Settlements has been in the Eurodollar market as a stabilizing influence.

I would like to say another thing about the Eurodollar market. I share the same worries that have been voiced around this table, but I agree with Professor Haberler that Eurodollars are "real" dollars; they are not a different type of dollar in the sense that, say, "investment sterling" is different from sterling for current transactions. It seems to me that there are only two important differences between what we call Eurodollars and ordinary dollars. The first is geographical. In the Eurodollar market, you do not need to go to New York; you can do all your business in London. Then there is another difference which, of course, is more important—the fact that European banks are sharing the function of creating dollar-denominated deposits. I think that this is as it should be, because Europe has been the banker of the world in a substantial sense: it has been providing net resources to the world. But Europe could not provide a world monetary instrument or standard of its own, so it has borrowed a monetary instrument from the United States.

JOHN EXTER: I have a small remark to add to this discussion on the lender of last resort in the Eurodollar market. I should like to point out that there is a difference in the Eurodollar market between lenders of last resort available to American banks and lenders of last resort available to non-American banks. The branches of an American bank in London are windows of a bank that is primarily a dollar bank with a long ladder of dollar assets and with access to the Federal Reserve System. In other words, for American banks, the Eurodollar market is just another source of dollar deposits. For a non-American bank in the Eurodollar market, the situation is very different. Let's take a sterling bank; its ladder of assets is principally in sterling, with a relatively small proportion of dollar assets, and it has no access to the Federal Reserve. So the liquidity problem and the lender-of-last-resort problem for a sterling bank or a Japanese bank or an Italian bank is quite different from the liquidity problem for an American bank.

I can give you an illustration at the time of the salad-oil case. Some British merchant banks had made loans to the salad-oil company; when the loans went sour, the banks had to meet their dollar obligations, and their recourse had to be to the Bank of England to get the dollars. I don't know—perhaps Sir Eric Roll can enlighten us on this—what the exact mechanics were; the banks may have used some of their sterling assets to acquire those dollars. This is a different kind of problem from the problem of an American bank. I may say that American banks could have a similar problem when they accept D-mark deposits, Swiss franc deposits, or other deposits denominated in foreign currencies.

JACQUES RUEFF: This discussion has been illuminating and most useful. I believe that there is a great potential danger in the huge mass of Eurodollars which could be converted into another currency, and I would therefore like to ask Professor Mundell this question—what are the steps which you think we should take in order to control the amount of Eurodollar currency?

MUNDELL: This is a very hard question, which I would like to answer, but I would like to think about it before answering.

Chairman THORP: I would agree that we hold this question, because it is clearly a central question that should be considered after we have attained our best possible understanding of the problem. In the meantime, several members have asked for the floor. The first is Mr. Silk.

LEONARD S. SILK: I shall be brief, because a number of the points that I wanted to make have already been made.

One thing that strikes me is that a new market mechanism has come into being for the simple reason that underlying economic factors have been more important than existing political arrangements. Why, with all the talk about European integration and with all the pulling apart there has been between America and Europe, should the dollar have played such an important role? The explanation, I dare say, is that a vacuum existed in the emerging European scene for an international money, and the fantastic thing is the speed with which dollars have rushed into that vacuum. It is a tribute in part to the ingenuity of bankers and of central bankers and to the vitality, still, of the profit motive.

I, too, feel that there are dangers here, and I would like to get more assurance that the experts understand the nature of the market before they try to control it. There seems to me to be a great deal of ignorance on how the market works, on where the money goes, on who is borrowing from whom; there is even this elementary question of who turns up in the market. Professor Machlup talked about Germans operating in the London market, and Sir Eric Roll, who inhabits that market physically every day, says that he has seen very few Germans there. Before one can control intelligently, one has to understand, and it seems to me that there is a fantastic degree of ignorance about the Eurodollar market and how it operates.

So I have the feeling, in comparing the situation with U.S. banking history, that we are about in the year 1847 and that we have to move rather rapidly along toward 1914 to establish some kind of Federal Reserve System which will understand the mechanism, preserve its useful features, and establish a reasonable degree of control.

ROBBINS: I am afraid that your proposal will strike terror into some British friends!

J. MARCUS FLEMING: I would like to point out that there is no necessary connection between the statistical discrepancy which Professor Machlup referred to yesterday—that is to say, the discrepancy between recorded official dollar holdings and the recorded U.S. liability to official holders—and the multiplication-of-reserve process which he explained in his address. Of course, I would agree with Machlup that this discrepancy—$13 billion in 1970—constitutes the bulk of the unexplained element in reserves. Let us suppose that $10 billion of this consists of the difference between dollar reserves, as recorded by non-U.S. monetary authorities, and official dollar liabilities, as recorded by the United States. That merely means that some central banks or other monetary authorities are holding dollars in the Eurodollar market—either directly, or indirectly through the Bank for International Settlements. It does not necessarily imply that there has been any credit expansion. I am not denying, of course, that there has been some expansion of a sort which could create extra dollar reserves, but the statistical discrepancy about which we are talking does not imply this necessarily.

Let me give one or two examples. If the German central bank switches from holding dollars in New York to holding them, either directly or via the BIS, in the Eurodollar market, and if the Euromarket continues to hold the dollars in the United States, then clearly the discrepancy in question will have appeared without any expansion of credit or of reserves. Rather, there will be a corresponding decline in the official-settlements deficit of the United States. One could argue that this decline in the deficit gives a false impression, and that the true size of the deficit would be obtained by adding in again the amount of Eurodollar holdings of central banks.

This is one case. The second is the same as the first except that the banks conducting the Eurodollar business decide that, instead of holding their assets in the United States, they will lend them out in Europe. Let's suppose that they lend them to some European firms which do not cover the exchange risk. What the firms want, of course, are European currencies, so the dollars flow into central banks, which count them as additional reserves. This is the case which was illustrated yesterday by Professor Machlup. Here you have no change in the U.S. official-settlements deficit and an increase in European reserves which has a slightly phoney character—at any rate, the increase does not constitute a claim against the United States; it constitutes a claim by one set of Europeans on another.

There is a third possibility, which is like the second case except that the firms which are borrowing from the Eurodollar market are covering the exchange risk. If they do that, then we have to consider two possibilities. One is that the counterpart is found by some bank which holds more assets in the United States in order to cover the foreign liability, in which case it becomes similar to my first case. The other possibility is that the movements in exchange rates evoke a certain amount of counterspeculation—that is to say, induce someone who is attracted by the premium on forward dollars to sell them forward and thus take the exchange risk. This case then becomes exactly the same as my second case.

We have these two basic cases; they are rather different in the way one has to look at them. What is their relative importance? I should have thought that in a year like 1969, when American banks were so anxious to get funds, the first alternative would have been more common, accompanied by an apparent decline in the U.S. deficit and no multiplied expansion of reserves. But in the circumstances that we have had in 1970 and 1971, when interest rates have been more attractive in Europe than in the United States, the second alternative would be more likely to prevail—though, to the extent that Eurobanks felt they had to have some kind of reserve in the form of a claim on U.S. banks, you would have an example of the first case again.

Of course, the expansion of dollar lending by Eurobanks does not have to start with a switch on the part of the central banks at all. There may, indeed, be a considerable switch—as there has been, no doubt, on the part of commercial banks—from holding claims on the United States to holding dollar claims in Europe. But that does not tend to provoke the discrepancy that we were talking about. Its effect is to expand the U.S. deficit and to expand the volume of international monetary reserves, but it does not account for this discrepancy. The discrepancy comes solely from decisions of the central banks to hold their assets in Eurodollar form rather than to hold them directly in the United States. And in some circumstances but not in others, as I have shown, you will have this multiplied expansion of reserves that Fritz Machlup was talking about yesterday.

ROBERT T. PARRY: Professor Mundell has expressed concern that if the United States went through another period of tight money, we might have a repetition of the 1969–70 Eurodollar experience with high interest rates. I wonder if this is true. We saw the suspension of Regulation Q in June and, at that time, were given a definite indication by the Federal Reserve System that it was not pleased with the operation of that regulation and would therefore presumably be very reluctant to reimpose it. This would suggest that the monetary authorities might provide a different source of funds for banks in a future period of tight money. My second point is that the regulation regarding reserve requirements against Eurodollars that took effect in January of this year probably means that borrowing by commercial banks in the Eurodollar market would be far more expensive in a future period of tight money than it was in the 1969–70 period. These two considerations suggest to me that the Federal Reserve would be very reluctant to allow history to repeat itself according to the 1969–70 pattern.

MARCELLO DE CECCO: I want to call attention to what we might call the microeconomics of the Eurodollar market—in particular, to examine the question of who holds deposits there. A great share of the deposits are owned by international corporations. The reason why international corporations need Eurodollar deposits is that, since they plan their operations on a world scale, they need an instrument which has world liquidity and is not subject to all sorts of restrictions by national authorities. The fact that most of the international corporations—in the neighborhood of 75 percent—are under U.S. control means that the U.S. monetary authorities have a very direct way of controlling the Eurodollar market. When the monetary climate changes in the United States, the American international corporations determine the climate in the Eurodollar market.

Looking at the matter from this point of view, I don't think
that all these remarks about impending doom are justified. If they
are justified, you can pin the doom to somebody's lapel, and that
somebody is the central bank—or, to put the matter another way,
the problem is the failure of central banks to agree on what should
be done. My conclusion is that there is a capacity to control, and
that if a control does not exist, that fact is clearly a policy; it is a
choice on the part of the monetary authorities.

SWOBODA: Let me also voice some doubt about impending
doom. I would agree with Professor Mundell that there are problems in controlling the Eurodollar market, but I see no reason to
believe that they are insoluble. Neither do I think that the system is
necessarily explosive. The situation is not that different from the
analogy Bob used of the country banks in the United States—of
one group of private banks using the deposits of another group of
private banks as high-powered money. That kind of system is not
necessarily explosive as long as there are reserve ratios that are
maintained and that may depend in some way on interest rates.

MUNDELL: But isn't that the point—that in the Eurodollar
market there aren't these controls that exist in the United States?
Country banks in the United States keep deposits in New York
banks which form the reserves for an escalation of credit, but the
situation is under the control of the Federal Reserve System,
which keeps a close eye on reserve ratios and other relevant
variables. The reserve ratio for country banks is different from the
reserve ratio for city banks, and these ratios are altered with
changing conditions. In the Eurodollar market, these controls
don't exist. When I talk about the explosive potential of the system, I do not mean that the system cannot be controlled; I haven't
answered Monsieur Rueff's question yet. What I mean is that the
system is not controlled at the present time and that there is no
present mechanism for controlling it.

SWOBODA: My one reservation would be simply a question of
ignorance on my part; I am not sure that there is no mechanism
for controlling it.

Chairman THORP: Well, I think there is a difference between
whether the system will explode and whether it is explosive. I
think we ought to give a few minutes to Fritz Machlup, who got
us into this problem.

MACHLUP: I hope I can say what I want to say in a few minutes. I would like, first of all, to ask you to distinguish sharply between (a) the creation of bank deposits of nonbank depositors in the Eurodollar market and (b) the creation of official dollar reserves in excess of the recorded U.S. liabilities to official foreign holders. These are two entirely different matters. True, in both cases there is some sort of duplication or multiplication involved, but the multipliers are of a very different nature and the mechanisms are very different. I ask you, therefore, to keep these two problems apart.

I believe that Gottfried Haberler exaggerates the importance of Regulation Q and the American capital controls. It is true that the expansion of the Eurodollar market in 1969 may largely be attributed to these measures, but the Eurodollar market could have developed without them, and it would continue if they were abolished. Regulation Q has already been suspended, and if the capital controls were also abolished, this would not mean that the Eurodollar market would disappear; I believe it would survive.

I think the comment yesterday by Sir Eric Roll and today by Leonard Silk about my example of a German borrower in London is really not quite relevant, as the nationality of the borrower is of no particular importance. It might just as well be an Italian borrower, and you would have the same consequences. But there is no reason to doubt that Germans have borrowed dollars in London.

Professor Swoboda and others have raised the point that it is quite possible that, as Eurodollars are created, some national deposits are destroyed in the process, so that Eurodollar deposits take the place of some honest domestic money supply. This is quite possible, but that would not be a reason for not counting this stateless money, because even if it is deducted from national money supplies, it is still part of the world money supply.

I do not think, however, that there has been merely this kind of replacement; I am quite sure that there has been a large amount of net money creation via the Eurodollar market. No one knows what the multiplier has been, if we can talk of a multiplier; more simply, no one knows how much money has been created. Some people have estimated the multiplier to be very low—perhaps just a little bit over one. Others have talked of a multiplier of two, or in that neighborhood. I believe that Eurodollar creation has been higher than this and, after the appearance of my article of September

1970 in the *Quarterly Review of the Banca Nazionale del Lavoro*, I found that at least two central bankers have accepted my theory that there may have been quite a bit of net money creation through the operation of the Eurodollar market. One was Governor Carli, who wrote an article in which he presented a model and some examples, and the other was Governor Stopper of the Swiss National Bank. I have in front of me a speech made by Governor Stopper, in which he says that he has no proof of how much monetary expansion has taken place, but that he believes the system definitely has the capacity to create money and that this capacity has actually been utilized to a considerable extent.

I agree with Marcus Fleming that the discrepancy between the dollar holdings now possessed by the monetary authorities of the world and the recorded U.S. dollar liabilities to official holders does not prove that the dollars placed by central banks have been returned to the central banks and have led, therefore, to a duplication of these dollars. The question is, who holds the New York dollars? If the central banks place New York dollars with the Bank for International Settlements, and the BIS places them in London and elsewhere, who holds them?

There are several possibilities. First, the dollars may be returned to the United States through normal transactions in the balance of payments. Second, the dollars may flow into the so-called outside areas—areas outside the eight countries that figure in the BIS statistics of the Eurodollar system. Third, the dollars may flow back to the central banks that have placed them with the BIS. A fourth possibility is that the dollars remain in the Eurobanks. Now the fact is that the New York dollars are not being held by the Eurobanks; the sum total of New York deposits held by Eurobanks has been estimated to be at most not more than 3 percent of their total dollar assets, with some estimates putting the figure at only 1 or 2 percent. It does not seem reasonable to me to assume that the backflow of dollars to the United States through normal payments has been as high as 97 percent or to assume that the flow to outside areas has been very large. I therefore conclude that the backflow to the central banks themselves has been considerable, though I do not pretend to know the exact amount.

I now come back to the question raised by Lord Robbins. The lender of last resort usually helps only the banks of its own jurisdiction. In the Eurodollar market, the branches of American banks

are perhaps the largest holders and lenders of Eurodollars. For
them, the Federal Reserve would be a lender of last resort. But
this does not hold for all the other European banks; they would
have to turn to their own central banks, and whether these central
banks would help them, either in domestic currency or in dollars,
is a question which at least has to be raised.

Chairman THORP: Before terminating the discussion on the
Eurodollar market, the chairman would like to introduce a minor
element in the picture which has not yet been mentioned. Since
the Eurodollar market was described as, among other things, a useful device for international corporations which have to operate in
many countries, I would like to insert the footnote that, as far as
the United States is concerned, the role of controller in these
corporations has become more than just one of making sure that
there are proper vouchers for all expenditures. Controllers now
spend much of their time trying to see that idle funds are part of
the profit-making assets of their institutions. They were among
the earliest people to become familiar with the Eurodollar market
and to make use of it as a way of earning their salaries—a task involving intimate familiarity with movements in interest rates as
well as with prospective changes in exchange rates.

But wait—another banker has asked for the floor: Mr. Jamison.

CONRAD C. JAMISON: Like many others, I have been a bit
uneasy for years about certain aspects of the Eurodollar market;
and Professor Machlup's comments, as well as those of some others
here, have accentuated my uneasiness. Machlup's credit spiral goes
round and round, with no apparent limitation on the number of
times it can do so.

All this is very disturbing. Whether the spiral works or doesn't
work in the way Professor Machlup has described, I wouldn't be
in a position to say, but since no one has seriously challenged
his analysis, I presume that it is substantially correct. It brings to
my mind the vision of the Sorcerer's Apprentice, and I wonder
who is going to turn off the machine.

If anyone is inclined to express serious doubts about Professor
Machlup's conclusions, I think we should hear from him, because
the subject is clearly important. We seem to be confronted with an
engine of inflation involving the creation of stateless money on an
alarming scale—a dangerous situation, since there is no international
authority to regulate or control it.

WALTER S. SALANT: My comment concerns the statements made about the lender of last resort. If there is interbank lending among banks operating in the Eurodollar market, and if non-American banks may borrow from an American bank, it would appear to me that the fact that the American bank has access to Federal Reserve means that Federal Reserve, in effect, is or can be lender of last resort for the entire system. So until I am corrected, I question the proposition that the Eurodollar market lacks a lender of last resort.

Chairman THORP: We now return to Professor Machlup, who may want to deal with this matter first.

MACHLUP: On Mr. Salant's last point, I would say that, when faced with a liquidity crunch, banks can sometimes borrow funds from banks in other countries, which in turn can count on help from their central banks. But events have not always worked out this way, and we cannot be certain that the Federal Reserve System can be relied upon as a lender of last resort for the entire world. It certainly was never assigned this function. The matter would depend very largely on Federal Reserve leadership—in particular, on whether the Federal Reserve would be inclined to help a particular bank, or group of banks, that was heavily engaged in helping banks in other countries.

SALANT: I think that if there were danger of a collapse on the scale that some of our members fear, the Federal Reserve System would not, to use Arthur Burns's words, "sit idly by."

MACHLUP: I share your hope! To change the subject, I think that Monsieur Rueff deserves an answer to his question on what possible controls might be advisable. Here we should distinguish between the creation of bank deposits held by nonbanks and the duplication or creation of official reserves. I will begin with the latter question—that is to say, what kinds of control would prevent the creation of official dollar reserves? My answer would be that the simplest procedure would be an agreement among central banks, possibly through the International Monetary Fund, that they will no longer invest their dollar reserves anywhere except perhaps with the Federal Reserve Bank of New York, which should of course pay a high enough rate of interest so that central banks would be willing to do that. I think this would solve the problem that has long disturbed Monsieur Rueff. In other words, the central banks that have received dollars from the U.S. deficit would no longer be able to invest them in any way except in an account with the Federal Reserve, and thus would not be increasing the lending capacity of American commercial banks.

HABERLER: You're restoring the gold standard!

MACHLUP: This would do what Monsieur Rueff wants. We would actually again have an automatic adjustment mechanism in which an outflow of dollars from the United States would reduce the reserve base of U.S. commercial banks.

RUEFF: I am happy to agree with the statement of Professor Machlup.

MACHLUP: So much for official reserves. In this case, we certainly would no longer have the possibility of investing dollars with the BIS, and thus would avoid the situation where the BIS places the dollars in London banks, the London banks give them to another borrower, and the borrower resells them to someone who might, directly or indirectly, return them to a European central bank. That would definitely be out.

HABERLER: Your proposals have nothing to do with the Eurodollar market.

MACHLUP: They have very much to do with the Eurodollar market, because, as I said before, the placing of official reserves through the BIS in the Eurodollar market certainly increases the lending capacity of the Eurobanks.

Let me proceed to the question of whether there is any way of controlling credit creation by the Eurobanks. Of course, the Eurobanks may say that they are not creating credit, but this is an old story; for over a hundred years, no American bank knew that it, in cooperation with all the other banks, was actually creating credit. The question is, can this credit creation be controlled? We know that the central banks are very anxious to do this; we know that Carli, Stopper, Emminger, and others have said that we must find means of control in this area and have not yet found them. I do not have a plan to propose, but I can think of several ways of attacking the problem.

One way would be to establish reserve requirements for deposit liabilities of the commercial banks, including liabilities that are not denominated in the national currency. Thus a German bank, for example, would be subject to reserve requirements on all deposits, whether denominated in D-marks or in other currencies.

Another possibility would be a procedure that the Swiss have been using. The Swiss have had very little control over their banks. In the last two years, the Swiss National Bank has decided that reserve requirements would be ineffective. Instead, it has favored a direct control over credit expansion by the commercial banks, limiting the expansion to certain percentages. During the past twelve months, the average limit was 9½ percent per annum.

There is a third possibility of control through the Federal Reserve System in the United States; but, frankly, I have not thought about it and I don't think I should dare to suggest how it could be done. I will only say that I believe that it could be done if we really wanted it and thought hard enough about it.

Before I conclude, let me say that I would not want to be on record as having proposed such controls. We do not yet know enough about the Eurodollar market to say how it should be controlled, if at all. We have to learn more about it; we know practically nothing because we do not have enough statistical information—in particular, we do not know enough about the composition of dollar assets and liabilities of the European banks. We have limited information for banks in London, but we have no information on the composition of dollar assets of Swiss banks or of the banks of any other European country. Thus I am doubtful that we should embark on a system of controls and regulations before we know the facts. On the other hand, I believe that it wouldn't be so difficult to obtain these facts if we really wanted to do so; and I feel strongly that the national authorities, at long last, should find out how the Eurodollar system really works.

MUNDELL: I should now like to reply to Monsieur Rueff's question concerning control of the Eurodollar market. I agree with Professor Machlup that the market can be controlled; and this conclusion reduces some of the fear of an impending collapse of the system as a whole. But I also agree with Professor Machlup that the dangers of control may be very serious, because the controllers may do the wrong things. It isn't quite clear what global monetary policy really should be, or even what the appropriate rate of global monetary expansion should be.

The system hasn't been controlled yet, in part because it is extremely profitable. The system is obviously not only creating great profits for banks but also performing a tremendously useful service.

The commercial banks are doing for the international community what the national central banks, for political reasons, have not been able to do. That is to say, they have been creating a world money. There is a gap in our present world system which John Parke Young discussed yesterday in a very thoughtful statement; that gap is the absence of a world currency. And what has been happening in an unplanned fashion is the rapid evolution of the U.S. dollar as a world currency.

Of course, this fact gives a great political influence to the United States in the control of the system. In an article for the *Journal of Money, Credit, and Banking* in August 1969, I recommended the formation of an Atlantic and Pacific Monetary Committee—a monetary council. This was an extension of Professor Kindleberger's recommendation that European central banks be added to the Federal Reserve Open-Market Committee. I don't regard that as a long-range reform, but simply as a transitional device toward the creation of a world currency. I think we are moving very rapidly—at a pace no one ten years ago could possibly have imagined—toward the need for a world money. And that world money should not be created or controlled by commercial banks; it should be created and controlled by government.

On the international level, the growth of multinational banking is closely connected with the growth of the multinational corporation. The annual expenditures of some of these great corporations are larger than those of many national governments. Kindleberger once said at a conference in Portugal (jokingly, but it was not completely a joke), "Who do you expect will be here in a hundred years—France or General Motors?" That was in jest, but we can be sure that the world we are moving toward, whether we like it or not, is going to be very different from the world we have now—and in ways that we cannot now completely comprehend or anticipate. But in the near future, I do think that something of the nature of an Atlantic Monetary Council would be a step toward a system in which control is not awarded, by default, to the United States. I don't think it is fair for the U.S. Federal Reserve System to manage the world money supply unless it has been given the authority to do so by other countries.

In any case, we have various alternatives. First, of course, we can simply do nothing, and let the system evolve along its own

lines. Second, we can move toward European monetary integration, perhaps creating a dual set-up, with a European money and
the dollar as separate systems. Third, we can move toward an
Atlantic solution as an interim approach toward a global arrangement. Some people look on European monetary integration as a
means by which European central banks and governments can acquire a bigger voice in an Atlantic framework—as a means of shifting some of the overwhelming power from the Federal Reserve
System and from the United States itself. They would like to create
a rival that makes it more interesting for Americans to say, "Well,
let's get together and work out an Atlantic or global system." At
the present time, any concession by the Americans is a concession
that is gratuitous; they already have control of the system, so
whether we envisage an American system, a European system, an
Atlantic system, or a global system is very much a question of the
timing of different influences.

To return to Monsieur Rueff's question, I would say that the
Eurodollar market can be controlled technically, just as Professor
Machlup has pointed out, but whether Machlup's technical solutions are best is a matter that would take a great deal of discussion
and thoughtful research. But I feel strongly that we should move
toward the creation of an Atlantic authority. There is a lack of
authority and a power vacuum in Atlantic monetary policy which
is badly in need of correction.

Chairman THORP: I'm afraid the chairman has to withdraw
his efforts to limit the discussion at this point, because Gottfried
Haberler, Sir Eric Roll, and Bob Triffin want to speak. Against these
three, the chairman is obviously helpless. The first is Gottfried.

HABERLER: I can be very brief. There has been a lot of talk of
control of the Eurodollar market. I regard that as something of
very limited importance. The really important control is control of
the money supply of the United States. Fritz Machlup proposed
that the European central banks should put their dollars into
blocked accounts with the Federal Reserve. That would not improve the situation unless the monetary policy of the United States
were changed. Suppose we had these blocked accounts but at the
same time the Federal Reserve was pursuing an inflationary policy;
nothing would be achieved. What matters is the type of monetary
policy pursued by the United States. In the absence of appropriate

U.S. fiscal and monetary policies, control of the Eurodollar market seems to me a rather empty gesture.

ROLL: I shall also be very brief, because I only want to say that I am almost 100 percent in agreement with what Bob Mundell has said. I should be very sorry if the dangers to which we pointed in the early part of our discussion today made us overlook the tremendous evolution that is taking place. Bob has described this development very rightly and succinctly as the evolution of a world money and a world monetary system. The important thing—and this is where I agree with him—surely is not to try to go back and undo this evolution, but rather to try to cope with the real problems that it creates. To my mind—and this may sound very starry-eyed—here is once again an argument in favor of a world central bank and world authorities to run the world monetary system. However visionary it may appear, I have worked myself around to this conclusion via the Eurodollar market, though of course there are other arguments in favor of such a development. I pointed some of them out years ago, as well as last year in the Per Jacobsson Lectures. Bill Martin, than whom there can be no more practical person in this business, added his very powerful voice in the same cause. So more power to Bob Mundell!

ROBERT TRIFFIN: I simply want to express my wholehearted agreement with the last remarks of Professor Machlup, Monsieur Rueff, Professor Mundell, and Sir Eric, but with the footnote by Professor Haberler that simply blocking foreign-exchange reserves with the Federal Reserve System is not a full solution. I am sure that Fritz agrees with that also. I think that the solution toward which we have to go is to put some reasonable ceiling on the total accumulation of national currencies as international reserves.

Chairman THORP: Our final speaker on this topic is a banker who wishes to deal with the Eurodollar market from a broader perspective. Mr. Exter.

JOHN EXTER: I confess to having been a bit dismayed as I listened to the discussion yesterday on worldwide inflation, because I felt that all too little was said about what I consider to be the real problem—namely, a worldwide liquidity freeze. This morning, through our discussion of the Eurodollar market, we have talked about this problem of liquidity. I can only say that I am sorry that the discussion has been distorted by what seems to me an excessive preoccupation with Eurodollars. Eurodollars are only part of the total problem, as I shall try to point out. But I do think that the discussion has been extraordinarily useful, because it has brought Fritz Machlup, with whom I have a wide area of disagreement, very close to the gold standard. As Professor Haberler pointed out, he came within a hair of advocating a return to gold-standard disciplines when he proposed that central banks keep their dollar deposits at the Federal Reserve. I shall revert to that later. And Bob Triffin has come very close too, because he now wants to put a limit on central bank holdings of foreign currencies.

TRIFFIN: I always have.

EXTER: Well then, Bob, welcome to the club! If you take the next step, which I think should be that any remaining deficit should be settled in gold, then we have . . .

TRIFFIN: The SDR standard, not the gold standard.

EXTER: Then I must deny your admission to the club. But I should regard this whole session as having been extremely productive if Jacques Rueff and I, who have a wide area of agreement, have convinced Fritz Machlup of the virtues of the gold standard. He is awfully close. I should wish him many more years of productive teaching if this session should bring him to that conclusion.

I'm not going to give you my model of the system. I tried to do that at the Claremont conference, and any listener who wants my thinking on that subject can read it in Randall Hinshaw's latest book.[1] Before I go further, I would also like to say that I have understood Bob Mundell much better today, when he talked about the explosiveness of the system, than I understood him yesterday, when he was discussing the Phillips curve and came to what was to me the remarkable conclusion that we could increase employment by pursuing a tighter money policy.

Lord Robbins, in his very stimulating address yesterday, referred ever so briefly to the corporate problem of liquidity. Jacques Rueff understands that problem fully, but he tended to confine himself to the international liquidity problem, so I would like to say a few words about the system as a whole.

I have found in my own thinking that it has been extremely useful to distinguish between money and credit. In the system as we have it today, I should regard the only real money as gold; gold is

[1] *The Economics of International Adjustment* (Baltimore: The Johns Hopkins Press, 1971).

the ultimate liquidity, the ultimate universally acceptable money. Except for gold, everything in the system is credit—paper promises to pay, IOUs. I say everything except gold, but I must also except SDRs, for the SDR is not even an IOU; I would call it a "who-owes-you?". Incredibly enough, there is no obligor, nor even a firm promise to pay.

Now, in ordinary times, IOUs can be used as money for long stretches of time. But these are extraordinary times, in which the difference between an IOU and real money—gold—becomes more important. I pointed out at Claremont that we had entered a world-wide liquidity squeeze and that, in such a squeeze, people become concerned about the convertibility of paper credit into gold. Today, the central bank holders of dollars want gold, and I think it was Professor Haberler who pointed out that the German central bank alone holds more dollars than the U.S. monetary authorities hold in gold.

But the real problem, it seems to me, is our understanding of the creation of credit. Credit can be created by anyone. It is created every time anyone succeeds in getting anyone else to accept his promise to pay, his IOU. So we all create credit; we create credit when we go into a gas station and buy gasoline by using a credit card. There is a whole spectrum of credit, beginning with currency notes and demand deposits. These two have the most attributes of money, for they are most commonly used as a means of payment. But in the United States, there are many other forms of credit, including time and savings deposits, certificates of deposit, Eurodollar deposits, commercial paper, Treasury bills, bonds of all kinds, credit cards, consumer credit, and so on.

Inflation is caused by excessive credit expansion in one form or another and, once under way, it tends to have a life of its own. This is why, I think, Bob Mundell used the word "explosiveness." And inflation gets to a point where the credit expansion must continue to keep the system going. The credit expansion becomes excessive in our modern world essentially because central banks, in effect, underwrite it. They underwrite it with their own credit expansion, and finally reach a point at which they dare not stop. They become locked into an expansion which they cannot bring to an end without disastrous consequences. Then they lose control, for the system begins to create credit in its own ways, some of which I have just pointed out—Eurodollar deposits, commercial paper, credit cards, and so on. The point is that we do not need banks to create credit. I wish some graduate student would make a study of Ireland last year, when the banks were closed for six months by a strike. Yet inflation went right on; credit creation went right on. Checkbooks were unavailable from the banks, so printers printed them. The pubs became clearing houses.

There is a special problem in a highly developed system like ours, in that some of the credit and debt creation is long-term—bonds, mortgages, and so on. Here we run into the age-old maxim of finance: beware of borrowing short and lending long. The real problem is that debt in the world grows much faster than the economy grows during a credit expansion. In the United States during the past eleven years, private debt grew half again as rapidly as the gross national product. We live in societies that require us to service and repay our debts, but the time comes in a credit and debt expansion when creditors begin to think that some of the illiquid debtors cannot pay. At that point, the credit expansion has problems in continuing to grow. I am told that Disraeli said, "Confidence is suspicion asleep." I think that suspicion is beginning to wake up. If my analysis is right, although we are worrying about inflation now, the time will come when we shall have to worry about deflation.

Let me conclude by returning to the proposal made by Fritz Machlup. Should foreign central banks, as he proposed, instead of placing dollars with the BIS, lend them to the Federal Reserve, which would then sterilize those dollars? That would at least have the virtue of eliminating the foreign central bank contribution to credit expansion in the United States. But the real decision is whether the central banks should use their dollars to buy U.S. gold. A gold purchase would cause an actual contraction of the credit base in the United States and thus help to restore international equilibrium. This is the point that Monsieur Rueff keeps making over and over again. You do not accomplish a contraction merely by placing the dollars with the Federal Reserve; you simply check an expansion. This is why I say that Professor Machlup has come very close, but not all the way, to the gold standard when he makes the suggestion that foreign central banks should deposit their dollars with the Federal Reserve.

VII. OPTIONS IN THERAPY: INCOMES POLICY AS A REMEDY FOR COST-PUSH INFLATION

Sir Roy Harrod and
Members of the Conference

Chairman THORP: Speaking for the moment in medical terminology, I would say that, having thus far spent our time as experts in the difficult terrain of examination and diagnosis, we must now shift our attention to issues in the field of prescription and therapy. Therefore, I propose this afternoon that we make a complete break with the kinds of things we have been talking about, and consider what can be done to cure, or at least to alleviate, the malady of worldwide inflation. One of the prescriptions most widely advocated at the present time is "incomes policy"—particularly as a method of dealing with cost-push inflation. So, with no more ado, I shall call on Sir Roy Harrod to introduce that subject.

Sir ROY HARROD: The subject of this conference is inflation in relation to what can be done internationally about it. To my mind, what we have been talking about is quite peripheral to the problem of inflation that is simultaneously confronting a large number of countries. As I said yesterday, I don't think that inflation really has much to do with Federal Reserve policy and that sort of thing. For a considerable period, but in the last two years especially, the problem has been one of cost-push inflation. The economies of both the United States and the United Kingdom have been running somewhat under capacity, and yet those countries have suffered the biggest wage-price explosion, apart from wartime, that I know of.

What are we going to do about it? What we need, I think, is a conference in which every alternate place around this table is occupied by a labor-union leader—a conference in which our purpose is to see what can be done to stop this inflation. Labor is very sympathetic. George Meany has declared himself in favor of direct interference in prices and wages in the United States, and the Trade Union Congress in the United Kingdom has definitely pronounced itself in favor of an incomes policy. Of course, we ought to have some employers around the table too; they know much less about economics than the labor leaders, but they should be represented because their help will be needed in putting an end to the inflation.

Suppose we conclude, as I think we should, that we need an incomes policy. In what order should we implement it? What should be our main principles? If I were asked how I would conduct an incomes policy, I would answer that, each year, I would set a mandatory limit under which wage rates, on the average, could not increase by more than productivity had increased in the preceding year. If the productivity increase had been 4 percent in the preceding year, I would use 3 percent as a sort of permissive guideline, leaving a margin of 1 percent to provide a little flexibility in dealing with all the difficult problems of negotiation—but on the firm understanding that 4 percent would be the mandatory limit.

What about prices? You can have a price freeze for a limited period, but you can't permanently freeze prices in a competitive society, nor do I think that you should freeze profits; you want profits to be big in order to encourage investment. And labor leaders understand that. What I think you would need to do is to have some form of limit on dividends. My idea would be to have a flexible surtax on dividends, so that if, during a year, dividends shot up more rapidly than wage rates, you could do something about it. I would include with dividends things like bonus shares, rights shares, and so on; these should not go up, per unit of capital employed, more rapidly than wage rates. Wage rates, productivity, profits; that is what we should be discussing around this table instead of all this nonsense about money supply.

Chairman THORP: Thank you very much; we'll make you a committee of one to try to organize such a conference. But I don't advise you to undertake being chairman of it! Next is Mr. McClellan, who, as former president of the National Association of Manufacturers, has a different perspective on the subject.

H. C. McCLELLAN: While I am impressed by the comments made by Sir Roy, I must with sincere respect vigorously disagree with his thesis that the problem of "wage-price push" is merely a sociological phenomenon. I declare that it is economic. Workers demand more money with which to buy things; their leaders are under pressure to keep them happy; failing in this, the leaders get fired. And I cannot agree with Sir Roy that union leadership is willing to limit pay increases to increases in output per man-hour of work.

My conclusions are not mere speculation. I served as chief labor negotiator for my industry for ten years. Furthermore, I have held direct discussions with Mr. George Meany on this issue, and I believe that I am familiar with his attitude. It is no different from the attitude I have confronted with any union official with whom I have ever negotiated. I have never discovered any willingness on the part of labor officials to relate wage increases to productivity increases.

Even though several previous speakers have referred to the current rapid changes in wages and prices, I feel that we have not yet given sufficient emphasis to this subject. I believe the wage-price push to be one of the fundamental causes of the current international inflationary problem, and I shall explain why.

First, let's consider what regulates prices. In the United States, there are two very strong curbs on excessive price increases: first, a set of antitrust laws which effectively prevents companies from joining together to fix prices and thus extract excessive margins of profit; and, second, a combination of domestic and foreign competition which, under normal conditions, is exceedingly effective in restraining business from overpricing its products. In this connection, I would point out that, even in the best of times, industry reaps only a modest net profit on sales. That profit remains reasonably constant as a percentage of sales for the companies which are successful; an average of 5 percent or less is reflected in the record each year. Out of this percentage must come dividends to stockholders and the financing of future growth of the enterprises. Obviously, higher costs mean higher prices.

Now let's look at the forces which regulate wages. Labor unions in the United States are specifically exempted from the antitrust laws. As a consequence, competition between unions has largely disappeared. Furthermore, it is common practice among unions, particularly in the larger industries, to utilize the closed-shop form of contract. Under this pattern, as you know, employers may hire only workers who already belong to the union which represents the employees of the company. This practice provides enormous power for the unions, and that power—today more than ever—is being exercised to escalate wage rates in new contracts without the slightest regard for increases in productivity, comparable wages in other industries, or the inflationary effects thus created.

Let me illustrate with hourly wage rates in the construction industry, as reflected by labor contracts covering 1970, 1971, 1972, and—in some cases—1973. Notice how sharply these wage rates increase. For unskilled construction labor, the figures are as follows: $5.84 in 1970, $6.64 in 1971, $7.45 in 1972, and $8.39 in 1973; for cement masons: $7.42 in 1970, $8.04 in 1971, and $8.74 in 1972; for carpenters: $7.60 in 1970, $8.20 in 1971, $8.90 in 1972, and $9.75 in 1973; for painters: $7.71 in 1970, $8.01 in 1971, $8.31 in 1972, and $8.61 in 1973; for electricians: $8.02 in 1970, $8.42 in 1971, $9.72 in 1972, and $11.42 in 1973; for sheet-metal workers: $8.31 in 1970, $9.31 in 1971, and $12.06 in 1972; and for plumbers: $10.43 in 1970, and $13.11 in 1971 (when this contract terminates)—an increase of 26 percent in one year! For the year 1971, the lowest hourly wage rate in the construction industry yields an annual salary of $13,800, and the highest hourly rate—for plumbers—yields an annual salary of $27,268. We now pay unskilled workers—water boys and clean-up men—more than we pay our policemen, our teachers, and even some of our executives and professional men.

Recently, an official spokesman for the Department of Housing and Urban Development in Washington declared that wage increases in the construction industry alone could create $10 billion of inflation this year. Overall, wage rates in the United States increased by 7.1 percent in 1970; in the same year, according to the Labor Relations Year Book published by the Bureau of National Affairs in Washington, labor productivity increased by only 0.9 percent. Under such conditions, price inflation is inevitable.

From my vantage point, it seems futile indeed to design a remedy for current international inflation based only upon better money management and improved control of credit, important as these may be. If we fail to cope with the basic problem created by the current escalating wage-price push, it will be like holding down the lid on a boiling kettle as a means of controlling the steam. I urge that we either come to grips with this problem around this table or design a conference which will permit an adequate analysis of inflation at its source.

ARNOLD COLLERY: I would like to make a few remarks about incomes policy. Incomes policy is based on the assumption that inflation is of the cost-push variety. We were told yesterday that no one any longer could deny that current inflation was caused by cost-push—even people at the University of Chicago could no longer deny that. Well, I remain skeptical; I still believe that inflation, even in 1971, can be caused by excessive demand. The only evidence that has been presented to prove to us that the current inflation is caused by cost-push is that we observe, simultaneously, rising prices and rising unemployment. But I learned from reading David Hume and other classical economists that if you increase the money stock relative to resources and to population, the result will be inflation. These classical writers—I think Lord Robbins pointed this out yesterday—did not believe that inflation would happen instantaneously; David Hume always argued that if new money came into the realm, the first effect would be to stimulate trade and business activity. If that is true, what we would first observe when we stimulate the economy with new money would be an expansion of output and a reduction of unemployment, with perhaps not much price effect, but, as the process got under way, we would see rising prices and rising unemployment.

Thus I remain skeptical about the present inflation being basically of a cost-push character. Now if our real problem is demand inflation, I think we can all predict that any incomes policy is going to be a failure. This leads me to wonder about how incomes policies have worked in the past. We had one in the United States in the mid-1960s; it may have been a rather weak policy, but it failed. It just did not work; we gave it up. In the United Kingdom, this approach has been tried a couple of times, and it failed.

HARROD: What do you mean? In 1948, we had an incomes policy in the United Kingdom. Unfortunately, it was abandoned for quite extrinsic reasons. There was a devaluation and a Korean War, and those two things killed the policy. But we were able to keep wage increases down to 2 percent a year for two years by deliberate policy—not by checking the money supply.

COLLERY: I would accept the proposition that an incomes policy could have a short-run effect on wages. The question is for how long—three years, five years, ten years?

HARROD: Our policy succeeded for two years, and would have gone on succeeding but for the two major events I have just mentioned—the Korean War and the devaluation of sterling.

COLLERY: I would like to make one more point. Even if it were true that we were experiencing cost-push inflation, I would be very skeptical about the prospects for getting together a group of labor-union leaders and asking them to be reasonable. I think what they would all say is, "Yes, of course we must not demand excessive wages, but my workers are underpaid, and all we want to do is to have a relative increase in wages in our sector; if other workers will behave themselves, there will be no problem." The fight over wages is very largely a fight over relative wages; and how you get union leaders to agree to accept some norm, such as that their wages shall not increase faster than productivity, I cannot imagine. Indeed, if the leaders were to accept such a norm, I am sure that the members would throw them out and get people who were more militant.

HARROD: Well, I don't know how many conferences of labor leaders you've been to, but I find the leaders extremely reasonable when you get them together.

COLLERY: Yes, of course; they know what they are supposed to say, but the question is—how do they behave?

Chairman THORP: I think we should turn this research problem over to a subcommittee of the National Research Council. I'll now call on Mr. Salant.

WALTER S. SALANT: Until this afternoon's session, we had, as I understood it, two theories of cost-push: Sir Roy's statement referring to sociological causes and Professor Mundell's explanation that wage increases are due to past price rises. Mr. McClellan has now added the influence of the closed shop and other monopolistic features of labor unions, and Professor Collery has just concluded that cost-push is really a monetary matter.

Well, with regard to both of these last two views, it seems to me that they don't account for what appears to be a new fact. After all, the monopolistic aspect of trade unions and the inflationary effect of undue monetary expansion are nothing new. But it appears to me that it is a new fact to have for so prolonged a period in at least two countries—the United States and the United Kingdom—the co-existence of rising prices and rising unemployment.

This leads me back to the two theories put forward by Sir Roy and by Bob Mundell, both of which are consistent, it seems to me, with this new situation. I would like to ask Bob how he would distinguish from the evidence whether his view or Sir Roy's view of the cost-raising influence is correct, whether the two theories are mutually exclusive, or whether perhaps both are operating. I raised this question with Bob yesterday during the coffee break, and I hope he will expand on the answer he gave me then. He said, "Well, that was all settled in the 1950s." But it's not clear to me how anything in the 1950s could settle what seems to be a new set of facts. We haven't before had price rises lasting a year or two after aggregate expenditure has fallen. So I would like to have Bob's opinion on what evidence would throw light on the question of whether Sir Roy's or Bob's theory is ruled out by the facts.

Chairman THORP: Do you mean you want Bob to answer whether or not the theory he presented is right? I think I can tell you what he'd say!

SALANT: No, I want him to tell me what sort of evidence would enable one to choose between these two hypotheses, because we are presumably not merely putting forward pet theories but are trying to find out what is in fact correct. Maybe the answer is that there is not sufficient available evidence, but what evidence would Bob want if it were available?

Chairman THORP: Let me restate your question so that it may not take quite so long to be answered. Are these two theories mutually exclusive, or could both be true?

SALANT: My question is, how would you know? And if the two theories could both be true, what facts would enable you to tell which was the preferred hypothesis?

ROBERT A. MUNDELL: I can give a quick answer to that, which also concerns what Mr. McClellan said. In 1930, when there was mass unemployment, people said that the unemployment was due to labor unions and to monopolies. Now during this inflation, people say that the inflation is due to labor unions and to monopolies. Well, the check is to see whether labor unions have become more powerful and to see whether monopolies have become more powerful. I do think that the issue was to a large extent settled in the 1950s, but that people have short memories. I have also looked at the evidence for Sir Roy's view, and find it completely wanting. When I hear Sir Roy saying that the cause of inflation is the environment, crime, permissiveness, and so on, I see these things far more as a consequence than as a cause of inflation. Inflation causes immorality.

I promised a short answer. The evidence seems to me perfectly clear. The question is simply: has there been an increase in the degree of unionization or of industrial concentration in the United States in the past five years? I have looked at the evidence, and the answer is no. And the alternative question, to support the monetarist view, is: has there been an increase in the rate of monetary expansion in the past five years? I have looked at the evidence, and the answer is yes.

SALANT: May I say that I started out by rejecting the explanation that cost-push is due to union strength and to monopoly. I asked you to distinguish, not between that explanation and the monetary explanation, but between Sir Roy's theory and the monetary explanation. I agree that cost-push is not explained by an increase in the power of labor unions or of industrial monopolies, and I grant you that the increase in the money supply has been a factor. I am sure that the price-level rise which has occurred has been a factor in the wage demands of labor unions; I don't want to be unsympathetic with your hypothesis.

MUNDELL: Why didn't you get cost-push inflation in 1960–65?

SALANT: Well, I'm not taking a position, but asking a question; one can't always assume that a person who asks a question has his own answer—sometimes, when he asks a question, he really wants to know the answer, incredible as that may seem. You have cited something which has occurred recently which did not occur in the early 1960s. That is a possible explanation. But Sir Roy has also cited something occurring now which did not occur in the early 1960s, so I still ask the same question; I would like to know.

MUNDELL: But differentiate. Sir Roy's sociological argument is similar to the position taken by the OECD—that inflation in the eighteen OECD countries could be explained by special factors operating in each of these countries. In other words, according to the OECD, there was no common cause of the inflation. That's absurd.

SALANT: I agree. But Sir Roy has pointed to something which is common to all the inflations.

Chairman THORP: Again, time is fleeing, and I fear that we must now set this argument aside, since several members want to talk on other matters. The first is Marcus Fleming.

J. MARCUS FLEMING: I don't know whether I'll even try to answer the question Walter Salant has raised, but I very much disagree with Sir Roy's view that everything we have discussed up to now is irrelevant to the problem of inflation. On the other hand, I do agree with Sir Roy that there has been an increased importance to this cost-push element in recent years, and I think I would try to reconcile these remarks by saying that there has been a deterioration in the short-run trade-off between unemployment and inflation. We are talking now about the Phillips curve, which Bob Mundell scathingly criticized yesterday.

I don't think one has to be quite as scathing as all that. There has been some rather interesting econometric work done on the determination of price increases, attempting to explain them in terms not only of variations in the level of unemployment but of past rates of change of price increase and rates of change of unemployment. This gives rather good results for some countries, such as the United States and Canada. This type of explanation is of course not very sociological; it is very economic, and it has elements of Bob Mundell's view that price changes and price anticipations affect the situation. At the same time, this view is compatible with a fairly stable long-run relationship between unemployment and the rate of inflation. Certainly, I am not such a great believer in econometrics as to feel confident that even the long-term Phillips curve is absolutely stable, but I do think this is still an open question and I think the Phillips curve is still a useful tool of analysis.

If that is so, I would define the object of incomes policy as being that of altering this long-run Phillips relationship. That some alteration should be possible seems rather plausible, as the relationship is quite different in different countries. For example, it is rather bad in the United States, bad in Canada, not very good in the United Kingdom, and very good in Germany. So there are variations, and presumably there may be ways and means of trying to alter the relationship. In the International Monetary Fund during the last couple of years, we have taken increasing interest in incomes policy, if one thinks of incomes policy as covering various ways of influencing this relationship. It seems to me that there is a whole range of possibilities that should be carefully and patiently investigated in this field.

It is not merely a matter of whether outright measures of wage control and price control are effective or are required. There are arbitration systems that are applied differently in different parts of the world. There are different ways of organizing collective bargaining. There is the role of labor-market policy, which in some countries is carried very far indeed, trying to match jobs to men and men to jobs. There is the influence of antimonopoly legislation. Productivity growth of course is a factor; that, however, is perhaps getting a little outside the normal sphere of incomes policy. But I think it's a bit early to come to any conclusions on the subject, though provisionally there is one thing that I can't help being struck by, and that is that as far as one can see—and this is the OECD conclusion also—incomes policy in one or another of these forms seems to work very much better in small countries than in large ones. We have heard something about the optimum currency area; there is also perhaps such a thing as the optimum incomes-policy area. This optimum incomes-policy area is probably a bit smaller than the larger national states and, of course, very much smaller than the superstate that some of us are trying to create.

The conclusion I would come to in this matter is that a great deal depends on having the right objectives in this field. I think that, in some cases, systems of incomes policy have broken down, as in the Netherlands, because of an attempt to hold inflation down to a level where it simply was not compatible with world inflation under fixed exchange rates. In view of the unwillingness to abandon fixed parities, it was incomes policy that had to go.

HARROD: The Netherlands had to give up incomes policy because it joined the Common Market; it became part of a larger area.

FRITZ MACHLUP: A few years ago, I wrote an article on cost-push and demand-pull inflation, in which I concluded that very seldom do we have pure demand inflation or pure cost inflation.

We usually have both together, but we can at least conceive of theoretical models of each type of disturbance in its pure form.

As I see matters, there are three kinds of demand-pull inflation. The first is the *autonomous* variety, which means a demand inflation that starts without a prior increase in wage rates. The second is *induced* demand-pull inflation, where the demand increase has been induced by a prior wage push. The third is *supportive* demand-pull inflation, where the demand increase has been the effect of the government's attempt to avoid the unemployment that would otherwise result from the cost push.

I distinguish also three kinds of cost-push inflation. The first I call *aggressive* cost-push inflation, where an aggressive wage push occurs without a prior increase in demand. The second is the *defensive* wage-push variety, where unions demand a wage increase because of a prior increase in the price level—in other words, where the wage group is trying to maintain its real wages. The third is what I call *responsive* cost-push inflation, where the wage push is a response to the increased demand.

Now what is a *pure* demand-pull inflation? This starts with an autonomous increase in demand, without a prior increase in wages, and is followed by a responsive wage push. If there are trade unions, they will ask for higher wages; if there are no trade unions, wages will simply rise because of the competition for more labor at the temporarily increased profit margins. In both cases, a wage push will follow the demand pull. A *pure* cost-push inflation, on the other hand, would start with an aggressive wage push, which would lead to induced borrowing by employers having to pay the higher wages, which in turn would lead to a supportive demand pull by the monetary authorities, who of course would be trying to avoid the unemployment that would otherwise follow.

In actual fact, especially if you examine a long period of time, you find demand pull and cost push working in tandem, with a big wage push followed by a demand pull, followed in turn by another wage push, and so on. I believe that most past periods are better explained by demand pull than by cost push and, therefore, I partly agree with Professors Collery and Mundell. But I also agree with others that there are periods when an aggressive wage push is the most potent force in the picture.

Now you may ask for evidence. Evidence could settle this matter, possibly, if you had a pure wage-push or a pure demand-pull inflation, but it cannot provide the answer if you have a mixture or an alternation of the two. This leads me to the views of Sir Roy Harrod. Surely he would not contend that there could be a wage-push inflation, continuing year after year, if the quantity of money —pardon that dirty expression—were absolutely fixed. If we had a fixed amount of gold coins and nothing else, there could not be a lasting wage-push inflation; there could only be a wage push which would shortly lead to unemployment.

HARROD: The velocity of circulation in the United Kingdom has been going up for twenty years.

MACHLUP: At the same time, there has been a great increase in the quantity of money.

HARROD: But not nearly as much as the increase in the national income.

MACHLUP: I grant that, but I doubt that you can finance a continuing cost-push inflation for years merely out of an increase in the velocity of circulation. I have never seen that happen, and I don't think you can provide evidence of a single country in all history that has had a continuing price inflation with a fixed quantity of money.

HARROD: But no country has ever had a fixed quantity of money.

MACHLUP: That's exactly it; that's what I've been saying.

ALEXANDER SWOBODA: I agree with Professor Machlup on money supply. Why the money supply was increased is another question.

GISELE PODBIELSKI: I would like to say a few words about the incomes-policy issue. I am rather struck with the tendency in all discussions of this kind to single out individual causes, whereas in real life there are always various factors operating simultaneously, so that several policy solutions need to be applied. I agree completely with those here who say that a cost inflation could not continue indefinitely in the absence of accommodating monetary policies. But what we have experienced so frequently in the United Kingdom is that when we have succeeded in slowing down a demand expansion, we continue to have wage-cost inflation which

may last for some time. This sort of problem may not contribute
to world inflation, but it does cause considerable difficulties for
the country concerned.

SWOBODA: Let me say a word about cost-push inflation. In
Italy last year, average wage rates increased by 21 percent. That's
all very interesting, but what do we predict from it if we know
only that? Well, we could predict that prices would go up by 21
percent. But what do we see? We see prices going up by between
4 and 6 percent, depending on which price index we use—approximately the rate that prices are going up in the rest of the world. So
if one is trying to explain the rate of inflation in a small country, I
wouldn't choose the cost-push explanation as long as we have fixed
exchange rates, since it is impossible for a small country to have a
rate of inflation widely different from the rest of the world for any
length of time.

In this context, Marcus Fleming said that perhaps the optimum
incomes-policy area is a small country. Well, if the purpose of the
policy is to improve the labor market, lower the rate of unemployment, and shift downward the Phillips curve, that is true. But if
incomes policy is to be an instrument to fight inflation, then I
don't think the optimum area is small, since a small country under
fixed exchange rates has little influence on international prices.
This is confirmed, in a way, by Mr. Fleming's last remark about
what happened in the Netherlands, where incomes policy was
abandoned because it was inconsistent with world inflation under
a regime of fixed exchange rates.

MARCELLO DE CECCO: First of all, I want to register a small
protest against Professor Swoboda, who comes from Switzerland
and calls Italy a small country! But let me go back to Professor
Machlup. In his statistical presentation yesterday, Machlup compared the annual rate of increase in the money supply of the major
countries, and showed that at the bottom of the list is the United
States. On this basis, it would appear that the United States is not
as much of a culprit in the creation of world inflation as is usually
believed.

But you cannot really compare the rate of increase of the money
supply for countries which have very small and unspecified capital
markets with the rate for countries which have large capital markets. If I had to make a list of credit instruments for my country,

as Mr. Exter did this morning for his, I would have to stop after a couple of items. This of course means that the velocity of circulation for Italy is a completely different thing than for the United States. More specifically, a given rate of increase in the money supply can generate a much greater inflation in a country like the United States or the United Kingdom than in Italy or Japan. I feel quite certain that the big differences we see in the rates of money creation from country to country are partly explained by the big differences in the size and character of capital markets.

VIII. OPTIONS IN THERAPY: THE ROLE OF FISCAL AND MONETARY POLICY

Robert A. Mundell and
Members of the Conference

Without doubt, the most exasperating and perplexing feature of the present inflation is the coexistence of sharply rising prices with substantial unemployment. The problem here is that measures to correct inflation are likely to increase unemployment, whereas measures to correct unemployment are likely to increase inflation. This dilemma, for which neither classical nor Keynesian theory provides any clear-cut guidance, led to the most spirited debate of the conference, a debate triggered by Professor Mundell's vigorous attack on the then current fiscal-monetary "mix" in the United States. This controversy, which dominated the second afternoon, is reproduced in the present chapter.

R.H.

Chairman THORP: In their remarks on incomes policy and on cost-push inflation, all the speakers have referred in one way or another—pro or con—to monetary policy, so I propose that we now direct our attention specifically to the role of monetary policy in coping with world inflation. Since issues of monetary policy and issues of fiscal policy are closely related, I suggest that we broaden our discussion to include both topics. Our first speaker is Professor Podbielski.

GISELE PODBIELSKI: I would like to ask Professor Mundell a question on what he said yesterday about the respective roles of fiscal policy and of monetary policy. I recall an article he wrote on this subject several years ago, in which he prescribed fiscal policy for domestic purposes and monetary policy for international purposes. This is different from the conclusion he came to yesterday, and I would like some further clarification from him on the role to be played by fiscal policy and by monetary policy in a world faced with both unemployment and inflation.

ROBERT A. MUNDELL: As most of you know, I argued in 1961-62 that we should use monetary policy to achieve external balance and fiscal policy to achieve internal balance. For the world as a whole, this leaves one degree of freedom, because there are n countries, but only n-1 exchange rates, so that if n-1 countries balance their payments, the remaining country also has its payments in balance. Under the gold-exchange standard, the extra degree of freedom is taken up by the stabilization of the price of gold. Because the United States is in the unique position of buying and selling gold freely—in principle if not in practice—it has been argued by Professor Haberler and others that the United States should ignore its balance of payments under a policy of "benign neglect" and aim instead for a stable price level. I also argued that once, back in 1965, but I changed my position when I became convinced that the United States would not discipline itself sufficiently.

Now the question is, if all the other countries in the world use monetary policy for external balance and fiscal policy for internal balance, what does it mean if the United States suffers simultaneously from inflation and unemployment? Are monetary and fiscal policies independent policies or are they really the same policies? I argued yesterday that contrary to the usual interpretation, they are independent policies and that there is an appropriate policy mix for "stagflation." My present view is that, for a closed economy, we should use monetary instruments to affect monetary targets and real instruments to affect real targets. We should use tighter money in order to control inflation and an easier budget policy in order to reduce unemployment when both are occurring simultaneously. Tighter money puts a more severe discipline on labor unions and monopolies, thereby reducing inflationary tendencies, while if there is unemployment—an evidence of waste in the economy—a tax reduction, by encouraging the use of idle resources, will tend to increase employment and aggregate supply, thus helping to deal with both problems—unemployment and inflation—at the same time.

The evidence is casual but, I think, in favor of what I have said. Let me cite one illustration. In 1948, the U.S. economy was in the midst of the greatest peace-time inflation it has ever had; and in the summer of that year Senator Taft advocated, and put through Congress over the head of President Truman, a big tax cut. The tax cut was not inflationary; in fact, it was quickly followed by a recession. I don't argue that the tax cut caused the 1949 recession, but I am convinced that, by encouraging an increase in aggregate supply at that time, it did contribute to stopping the inflation.

Most people argue that a tax cut will be tremendously inflationary, and that is what I deny. Just remember that the $50 billion gap between actual and potential U.S. gross national product represents the possibility of a substantial increase in aggregate supply. Unemployment in the United States now is 5 million, a figure equal to the entire labor force of Belgium. This is much too large an inventory of potential work. I am not arguing that we can employ them all, because there will always be some turnover, but the idea of having 5 million people changing jobs is simply absurd; it is not necessary to set such low standards for stabilization.

Chairman THORP: Lord Robbins wants to make sure that you have more to say on this; he has a question to ask.

Lord ROBBINS: I am in a muddle about Bob's proposition. In the end, I nearly always agree with him, but I find some difficulty in generalizing what perhaps I mistakenly believe to be his general proposition. Perhaps I can put my perplexity in this way: Suppose you have a community which has just started a war—financed for the time being by monetary inflation—and then the government, listening to orthodox economists, imposes fairly heavy taxes; what, according to the Mundell doctrine, would be the effect of that? Would it be to increase the inflation or to diminish it?

MUNDELL: The question would turn on what happens to aggregate supply. An increase in taxes could cause a withdrawal from the exchange economy and a reduction in aggregate output, whereas bond finance of the war could generate an increase in aggregate supply. Taxation is a coercive means of releasing resources, whereas borrowing is voluntary—and that can generate very different supply-of-effort responses.

People tend to underestimate the elasticity of the capitalistic economy, to use an unfashionable expression. The tremendous potential of the economic system to adapt itself when demands are put on it is well illustrated by the enormous increase in productivity in the U.S. economy in 1940–42, when there was an immense expansion of output with only a very small amount of inflation. Of course, the expansion was partly made possible by the slack from involuntary idleness, but it was also due to an alteration of ideas and effort. In the United States at the present time, both capital and labor are unemployed; at least 25 percent of plant and equipment is underutilized and 5 million people are out of work. What is the purpose of higher taxes? We want to increase real effective demand, not diminish it. Now my assertion here is that easy money will simply bid up prices, whereas tax reduction will increase effective demand and encourage the employment of idle capital and labor.

Here we can learn a great deal from the Germans and the Japanese, both of whom have used tax reduction to good effect. The Japanese have had a program of systematic tax reduction involving periodic tax cuts almost every year since 1950. At the same time, the Japanese economy has had a growth rate of 12–14 percent a year over a twenty-year period. And the Japanese trade unions are not supposed to be powerful, but they have been getting wage increases—real-wage increases—of the order of 12–15 percent per year during this period. On the other hand, in the United Kingdom, where trade unions are supposed to be so powerful, wage earners have been getting real-wage increases of only 2–4 percent a year. Part of the explanation for this paradox involves the share of wages in the national income. In the United Kingdom, wages account for over 70 percent of the national income, whereas in Japan the figure a few years ago was only 53 percent and now, I think, is something like 58 percent. Japanese workers have accepted a low share of wages in the national income, together with a rapid rise in real wages, while British workers have opted for a high share in the national income in an economy where growth in all magnitudes, including real wages, has been discouragingly low.

Chairman THORP: Several members are eager to participate in this discussion of fiscal policy and monetary policy as methods of dealing with world inflation. The first is Gottfried Haberler.

GOTTFRIED HABERLER: I want to comment on the early postwar tax cut which Bob mentioned. His facts are perfectly correct. The tax cut was passed by Congress over the veto of President Truman, and the president had the support of practically all economists, who argued that since there still was inflation, the government should not cut taxes.

But then it turned out that the tax cut was the right thing to do—though for very different reasons from those that Bob mentioned. It turned out that, very soon after the tax cut went into effect, the first postwar recession set in, so the tax cut was perfectly timed to deal with that problem. This was not the foresight of Congress; it was just by chance. But I fully agree with Bob that if you have a tax system which is extremely progressive, you can get a long-run improvement in efficiency by stimulating investment through cutting taxes in the proper way. But this is a long-run affair; you could not expect short-run effects via that route.

From the short-run standpoint, Bob now has a new theory. His old theory was that fiscal policy should take care of internal balance, while monetary policy should take care of external balance. I have certain doubts about that, but let me concentrate on his new theory, in which he says that the short-run effect of a tax cut—not simply a budget deficit but a budget deficit brought about by a tax cut—is almost entirely on real GNP. More concretely, if at the present time in the United States taxes were cut, we could count on an increase in real GNP, with very little inflation. On the other hand, if we try to stimulate the economy by monetary policy, then all or most of the effect would be in the form of inflation. In other words, in the short run, tax cuts increase real GNP, increase productivity, and increase aggregate supply, without excessive inflation, whereas monetary expansion simply increases inflation. If I understand Bob right, the difference is that expansionary monetary policy immediately creates the expectation of rising prices, leading workers to ask for higher wages, so that the result is higher money wages and other money incomes, with little, if any, increase in real GNP.

But here my difficulties arise. I agree that if people read that monetary policy has become more expansive and that interest rates are going down, they will draw the conclusion that there will be more inflation. But if there is a large deficit in the budget brought about either by an increase in expenditure or by a reduction in taxes, it would seem to me that they are likely to draw the same conclusion. To build up such an important theory on the assumption that expectations will be different in the two cases seems to

me a very questionable thing to do. From a short-term standpoint,
I see very little difference between stimulating an economy through
easy-money policy and stimulating it through easy fiscal policy.
Both operate through an increase in aggregate demand. Monetary
policy would operate in the first instance on investment, whereas
tax cutting, depending on what kinds of taxes were cut, would
operate on either investment or consumption. Whether the initial
impact is on investment or on consumption is, I believe, rather unimportant, because in the next round this washes out.

Chairman THORP: Bob, I want you to receive all the arrows
before you speak so that you can deal with them all at once. The
next archer is John Exter.

JOHN EXTER: I would like to comment on Bob Mundell's comparison between the impressive performance of Japan and the un-
impressive performance of the United Kingdom. There are two
factors that occur to me immediately which are quite different
in the two countries. In the first place, Japan after World War II
had its indebtedness wiped out, so that the Japanese economy
ever since the war has been extraordinarily liquid. In the second
place, the Japanese currency has been undervalued in relation to
other currencies since 1948, when the yen was devalued. By way
of contrast, the United Kingdom came out of World War II in an
extremely illiquid position, both internally and externally, and,
during much of the postwar period, sterling has been overvalued.

Chairman THORP: Another banker has asked for the floor. Mr.
Magnifico.

GIOVANNI MAGNIFICO: As I understand it, a fundamental feature of Professor Mundell's theory is the concept of a full-employment budget—a maneuver already successfully employed in the
United States in the early 1960s. The matter was well illustrated
in a lecture by Walter Heller, in which he explained that if you have
an inflation of incomes, you will also have a built-in mechanism in
the tax system which will tend to choke recovery because of the
progressive tax-rate schedule. This observation is true, I think, and
from it one must draw the conclusion that you cannot rely on the
automaticity of the tax system; you have to do something of a dis-
cretionary nature—in other words, you have to manipulate tax
policies. Professor Mundell adds a new element by suggesting that,
in dealing with inflation, it may be better to lower taxes rather than

to raise them. I am not sure of this. I have doubts of the same kind which Professor Haberler has expressed, and am inclined to the view that it is difficult to fight inflation without having some support from a tighter fiscal policy.

SVEN W. ARNDT: Let me make a general comment on the Mundell theory. It seems to me that there is an argument in support of Bob's idea of coupling fiscal policy with the employment goal and of coupling monetary policy with the price-stability target; but it is an argument which, unlike Bob's, does not require special assumptions about expectations.

To illustrate what I have in mind, let us suppose that we are concerned with inflation in an economy in which industries are characterized by wide differences in their economic development, their use of technology, their response to general monetary and fiscal measures, and the degree to which they lead, lag behind, or are unaffected by, the business cycle. In such an economy, the national unemployment figure is an average which may conceal enormous differences from industry to industry and from region to region. This means that a general fiscal expansion which does not discriminate among industries and regions will be too little for some and too much for others. In such a situation, I would argue that selective policies are needed—notably selective tax incentives and subsidies for industries and regions hard hit by unemployment. I would agree with Professor Mundell that monetary policy should be used to achieve a stable price level, but I would argue that unemployment should be attacked, not by a general tax cut, but by selective fiscal policies designed to deal with possibly a wide variety of specific and localized situations.

Chairman THORP: Fritz Machlup has a question to put on the table.

FRITZ MACHLUP: As usual, Mundell has put a puzzle before us. I am trying to solve it, and I want to ask a question to see whether I understand it correctly. I should first acknowledge the help of Walter Salant who, during the coffee break, tried with me to solve the problem. Bob, is it correct that you mean that, for countries other than the United States, fiscal policy serves the employment purpose and monetary policy serves the purpose of maintaining external balance? If such countries balance their external accounts, the United States is also in balance and therefore is able to use monetary policy freely as another instrument. So in the United States, fiscal policy should be used to maintain full employment and monetary policy to stabilize the price level. Is that a correct interpretation?

MUNDELL: No.

ROBBINS: I think, Fritz, that your question does bring in possibly an additional way of escape. But, before coming to your question, I want Bob to face the question in a closed economy of the alternative effects of fiscal and monetary policies.

Chairman THORP: As far as I know, Bob, these are all the questions that you're called upon to deal with.

MUNDELL: The chairman's comment about catching the arrows puts me in the position of Saint Sebastian, who wasn't able to. Many arrows have been directed at me, and many issues are at stake.

First, let me make a couple of rather trivial comments on the matters raised by Gottfried Haberler. Gottfried's remark about the 1949 recession prompts me to ask about the turn of the business cycle, the postwar inflation, and the assumption that somehow both were inevitable. If I were asking a rhetorical question, I would say, who timed the business-cycle downturn? It wasn't inevitable; it was tied up with the policies of the United States. Another point which Gottfried made was that I am offering a new theory. It is not exactly a new theory; it is simply an application of theoretical knowledge to a new situation.

Fritz Machlup has asked me if I agree that if n – 1 countries use monetary policy for external balance and fiscal policy for internal objectives, the remaining country—namely, the United States—need not be concerned with its balance of payments but, instead, should pursue the aim of controlling world inflation. That was at one time my position, but now I feel that the United States has not shown itself to be a responsible enough financial leader to be given the sole responsibility for controlling the rate of world inflation. Thus there is a need to involve more sharing of that last n – 1 degree of freedom among a wider group of countries. After all, other countries deserve a more important role than simply as policy advisors to the United States.

Turning to Lord Robbins, I think that he is correct in saying that I should make my theoretical point about inflation and unemployment on closed-economy grounds. After all, the world economy is a closed economy, and we are talking about world inflation. Moreover, the U.S. economy accounts for over one-third of the world economy in terms of GNP; it accounts for roughly half the OECD economy, and my recommendations apply primarily to the United States, where the problem clearly is to correct unemployment while reducing the rate of inflation.

Now it is very cheap and easy to say that we have to tighten up on budgetary policy and tighten up on monetary policy; that may be great for world inflation, but it's awful for unemployment, which will increase if we move in that direction. Easier monetary policy will lead to more inflation, and I don't think it will reduce unemployment very much. So that policy is out. If, as Professor Haberler was arguing, fiscal policy operates in exactly the same way as monetary policy, there is no way out of the dilemma. If he is right—and it's the standard view—we can have more inflation with less unemployment or more unemployment with less inflation, but we can't get to a higher welfare position involving simultaneously lower inflation with full employment. So that's the issue.

Sir ROY HARROD: May I ask this: In a multicountry world, does your stabilizing system imply that a given country can balance its external position on the assumption of international capital movements, plus or minus, which may be large? The point of this question is that your monetary policy, as I understand it, influences capital movements.

MUNDELL: May I ask you to postpone that question, because there are enough issues to take care of at this point. I don't want to confuse matters by introducing the issue you raise, as I want to focus on a single issue, which is that if you have inflation plus unemployment, and if you have two policies—monetary policy and fiscal policy—can you correct inflation and unemployment simultaneously.

Now the question is, is monetary and fiscal policy one instrument or is it two instruments? And the basic theoretical proposition that I am making here is that we have two instruments, not one instrument, and that the two instruments can be used in opposite directions in order to achieve simultaneously a lower rate of inflation and a lower level of unemployment. The reason for this is that, in an economy like the United States that has developed inflationary expectations and where everyone reads the newspapers, a prime and immediate indicator of expectations is Federal Reserve policy.

Now I deny that this is a new phenomenon because, if I remember correctly, two famous English economists, Alfred Marshall and J. M. Keynes, made the same point. According to Marshall, in *Money, Credit, and Commerce*, one of the important matters affecting expectations in years back was whether gold was coming in or going out. An inflow of gold in the nineteenth century was an indication that credit would ease, with possibly inflationary consequences. In his *Treatise on Money*, Keynes emphasized monetary policy itself as an indicator of expectations.

This is certainly true in the United States. If Arthur Burns announces that the Federal Reserve is going to pump money into the economy in order to reduce unemployment, that will immediately have an effect on the capital market and on the economy as a whole. Lenders, expecting higher prices, will demand a higher yield on bonds; trade-union leaders will add to their demands for higher wage rates, perhaps not simply in proportion to the increase in the money supply but by a greater proportion, so that an expansionary monetary policy, far from reducing unemployment as would be predicted by a Phillips curve economist, may actually increase unemployment. This possibility is illustrated by empirical evidence from the Brazilian economy and also, of course, from the great inflations of the past. I think that almost every systematic inflation that has gone on for any length of time has indicated that monetary expansion is not a device for keeping unemployment down but, on the contrary, ultimately leads to an increase in unemployment.

There are two theories of what happens when you have an inflation. There is a theory which is popular in some branches of the U.S. administration that inflation must be followed by a recession or depression in order to get wage rates down. You create the recession by tightening up on monetary and fiscal policy; this puts a squeeze on the economy and reduces spending, so that prices start to fall, real wages rise, and employment falls. Eventually, after two or three years, the labor unions are disciplined and then are supposed to act like docile animals. Workers accept lower wages, and the rate of inflation is reduced to a more palatable level. That's the policy that was tried in 1968–70; it led to a recession, but it did not stop the inflation.

The other theory, which derives from Ludwig von Mises and John Exter, states that after an inflation a collapse is inevitable because of a liquidity crisis. Creditors become worried about the ability to repay of the more illiquid debtors, widespread bankruptcies occur, and inefficient firms get knocked out of the system. We had that experience in 1930–31, followed by a decade of depression. Our current recession has been a much shorter affair, but I would argue that neither the 1930 variety nor the current variety is necessary. I am not in favor of monetary contraction; instead, I am in favor of a careful doctoring of the economy which involves informing the public about what monetary policy is going to be and about the expected price level at which stabilization is going to occur, so that wage demands can be made in this context.

In this connection, there may be a possibility of getting more resources than you are currently producing. In an open economy—and here I come to Sir Roy's question about capital movements—you could get the resources by following a less expansionary monetary policy which, through a higher interest rate, would attract capital from abroad. This would allow the economy to have a deficit on current account which would increase the national supply of goods and services, thus providing a cushion that would permit the economy to adjust and to get into equilibrium.

HARROD: May I interrupt you? You say that there is time for adjustment because you have attracted capital by higher interest rates, but is there any mechanism in your system by which you would balance the external position?

MUNDELL: In a closed economy, which is what we were talking about earlier, you don't have access to international resources; the world cannot borrow from the moon. Bagehot said, didn't he, that an interest rate of 8 percent would attract gold from the moon; but the astronauts didn't find any, so you can't rely on that source. In a closed economy that is fully employed, there are no additional resources; you are already using them all, and stopping inflation under these conditions may be a very difficult problem. But if you have an economy that has substantial unused capacity and idle labor, then you can have that gold or green cheese from the moon by making use of the magic that Keynes discovered in 1936. In the U.S. case, you simply employ more people, you employ more capital, and you get the $50 billion in resources which is the analogue for a closed economy of the capital imports that might come into an open economy. You make the pie bigger by increasing employment; and the *sine qua non* of the increased employment is an increase in real effective demand, which can be achieved through a reduction in taxes. Of course, you might also get the increased employment through an increase in government spending, and I agree that this would be a useful thing, but you might not get the same favorable supply response. But leave that aside. The point is that you need the increase in effective demand, and you can get it through fiscal policy.

Gottfried Haberler said, "Ah, but that means a budget deficit." It may or may not, because the tax base, through multiplier and accelerator effects, may change. But suppose it does mean a budget deficit in the United States—who cares?

HABERLER: Then the money supply . . .

MUNDELL: Look, Gottfried, I've been listening to you parroting *my* remarks; can't you listen to me parroting yours? I'm frankly not worried about this problem at all. I think it's a mirage, and I think it's shocking that, thirty-five years after the Keynesian revolution, we should be squabbling about an issue that should have long been laid to rest.

So, to conclude, the proper mix for a closed economy that has unemployment and inflation is a tax cut combined with monetary restraint. The tax cut will employ more people and equipment, and the economy will move at a far faster rate toward recovery than before. The money supply would increase at a faster rate than it would under present policies, because the economy would be expanding at a faster rate. But it would be a controlled monetary expansion, resulting in an upward drift in the rate of interest.

J. MARCUS FLEMING: I feel that Bob still hasn't answered Gottfried's perfectly simple question—why should an expansionary monetary policy have more effect on prices than an increased budget deficit has? Is it alleged that the public is more allergic or sensitive to monetary policy than it is to fiscal policy? My second question is, if the system is that every country except the United

States has to use this rather inefficient weapon of fiscal policy for fighting inflation and has to devote monetary policy to getting its balance of payments right, while the United States has the choice of two policies to deal with two problems, does this not place the United States in an unduly favored position?

Chairman THORP: Walter, I'll give you the floor, but since you missed the first half of this discussion, I may have to tell you that you're repeating points that have been made.

WALTER S. SALANT: I'm going to try to avoid repeating what I deduce has already been asked. Let me ask you, Mr. Chairman, if the question was asked as to why a reduction in taxes operates differently from an increase in government expenditure; if not, I'd like to ask that question and hope for an answer, but if it's been answered, or asked and not answered, I won't ask it, because I probably won't get the answer either.

MUNDELL: One answer is the balanced-budget multiplier, which you probably had a part in inventing.

SALANT: My brother gets that credit. This view of Bob is quite a departure from the notion that monetary and fiscal policies are two ways of affecting aggregate expenditure, but it isn't clear to me what the mechanism is, despite Bob's effort to explain matters by saying that the nominal rate of interest is influenced by what everyone reads in the paper concerning the money supply. His observation would be correct, I think, if the level of the bond prices were wholly determined by people who study at the University of Chicago—and who believe what they study—plus those who believe the same things without having studied there. But I'm a little skeptical about that.

Another point I would like to raise is whether the monetary restraint that Bob supposes to affect prices, affects prices no matter how the money supply is restrained, or whether the restraint has to work through the market mechanism. Suppose you limit the money supply by rationing credit; would that avoid adverse effects on output? My guess is, No. If there were a general control of money supply through rationing of bank loans, some people might have to contract their operations even though their capacity was not strained, so that you might get a situation where some firms, owing to inadequacy of working capital, might have to contract output even though they were not bottlenecks—even though they had adequate supplies of labor and excess capacity. In that case, you might argue that if you then substituted the market mechanism for credit rationing, you would not get this bad distribution of credit—that the only ones who would be restricted would be those whose capacity was strained. In other words, you might argue that you would get more output if you restricted the money supply by the market mechanism than by rationing, because credit would be used more efficiently. But this argument involves, not a distinction between restriction via the money supply and restriction via fiscal means, but a distinction between two ways of restricting the money supply.

I could understand that theory, but I am not sure whether it is the one that Bob is putting forward. Something he said a moment ago led me to think that this is what he means, because he said that monetary restraint should work through the marketplace. And perhaps he means that wasteful kinds of capital expenditure would not be undertaken, whereas they might be undertaken when money supply was restricted by credit rationing. But it is not clear to me that this is what Bob is saying. Moreover, even if it is what he is saying, I wonder whether that mechanism can work fast enough to account for the short-period phenomenon he seeks to explain.

Chairman THORP: Bob, it seems to me that you should have the last word.

MUNDELL: Just a footnote—the University of Chicago did not invent the theory of appreciation and interest; this was first put forward by Alfred Marshall, but is usually identified—correctly, I think—with a very great American economist, Irving Fisher, who worked out the idea more fully. Unfortunately, Fisher was a Yale man. I did not understand Walter's last point; I'm sorry. It was a long point, but I didn't understand it.

SALANT: I was raising the question of whether the mechanism you have in mind involves efficient distribution of the money supply to individual firms through constraint on the money supply operating through the rate of interest.

Chairman THORP: The question is, would you get the same effects on output when you constrain the money supply through bank rationing that you get when you constrain the money supply through the interest rate?

MUNDELL: To simplify all that, we can skip directly to an old proposition about monetary and fiscal policy developed by John Stuart Mill. It is a very explicit statement that I think will answer this question. Does an increase in the money supply lower or raise the rate of interest? That's what we're talking about, isn't it?

SALANT: Are you talking now about the nominal rate or the real rate?

MUNDELL: The nominal rate. In Keynesian theory, an increase in the money supply lowers the interest rate; in classical theory, it leaves it unchanged. What did Mill say? He said that the answer depends on how the increase in the money supply comes about. If it comes about through an increase in government spending, the interest rate will rise. If it comes about through an increase in credit, the interest rate will fall. This view, I think, is by and large correct if we assume a given state of expectations. But with a state of expectations where monetary expansion is identified with an acceleration of the rate of inflation, the result will be a rise in the rate of interest in both cases, because people will sell bonds to an extent which will put an inflation premium on the return to those bonds.

Let me conclude with a comment on Marcus Fleming's last remark. I should say first that I used to work for Marcus at the International Monetary Fund. At that time, the IMF had a theory that monetary policy should be used to correct the internal economy, and fiscal policy should be used to correct the external balance. It was at that point that I wrote my article saying that this policy was wrong and that the policy mix needed to be changed, particularly in the United States. I argued that the U.S. economy needed a tax cut. Well, you all know what happened in 1961–63; the United States struggled along with 5½ percent unemployment until it got the tax cut finally in 1964. The tax cut was followed by a tremendous acceleration of the U.S. economy, and was a great success. But on the differential effects of fiscal and monetary policy, the IMF was wrong then, and I suspect it is wrong now, though I am not clear that the Fund has a theory on how fiscal and monetary effects differ.

What we need is a more realistic theory of expectations. The matter is tremendously complicated. Keynes, in *The General Theory*, regarded expectations as a volatile variable which shifts the marginal-efficiency-of-capital curve up and down, causing the business cycle. In this respect, Keynes was much more realistic than some of his followers, who built into their wooden models

the assumption that the state of the world is given and that expected future prices are constant. This has parodied the whole
Keynesian theory of effective demand, and has led to grave mis-
interpretations.

I won't give a complete theory of expectations at this time. I'm
simply saying that the theory that an increase in the money supply
will lead to an increase in expected future prices is better than the
theory that it will lead to constant future prices and leave everything else unchanged. That is all that's necessary in order to establish the basic point I am making here of the differential effects of
monetary and fiscal policies.

Chairman THORP: Since it's time for us to adjourn, the chairman will save Saint Sebastian from any further arrows.

IX. CONCLUDING OBSERVATIONS

Lord Robbins
Sir Roy Harrod
Jacques Rueff
Robert A. Mundell
J. Marcus Fleming
John Parke Young

Chairman THORP: Since this conference began, not only has a great deal been said around this table, but there have been various social and gastronomic events at which, in the midst of unanimous comfort and contentment, we have nevertheless proceeded to reveal areas of disagreement and of unanswered questions. So we have created over this period, as is the custom of conferences like ours, what I would call a considerable state of uncertainty as to facts and of at least apparent confusion as to their interpretation. Very fortunately, we have with us a person who has dedicated a great deal of his life to trying to find beauty in the apparent disorder which one sees in modern art and in modern music; and this is a splendid background for interpreting our conference. Accordingly, I call on Lord Robbins, our moderator, to review our deliberations with the aim of extracting whatever wisdom can be distilled from them.

Lord ROBBINS: Well, Mr. Chairman, I don't know that you have added to the clarification of the situation by your remarks. I must say that I think more highly of the observations of our colleagues than your comparison with the latest manifestations of the avant-garde, which consist of a few strands of rope thrown about the floor or an old pair of trousers hanging from the ceiling. Surely, the contributions of Sir Roy Harrod, Professor Mundell, and many others here have a higher status than that!

Indeed, I think that the difficulty of the assignment that you have given me is really a tribute to the excellence of the contributions. I can honestly say that I have never attended a conference which I have found at once more illuminating as regards technical detail and more thought-provoking as regards a wider horizon. I do sincerely, from the bottom of my heart, congratulate Grove Haines and Randall Hinshaw for the success of this get-together.

Now, coming to the survey, which, I apologize to you all, is going to take rather a long time—this again is a tribute to the weight of the matter which has been contributed—let me begin with an absolutely noncontroversial tribute to Fritz Machlup. His factual survey the first morning of our meeting did a great deal to get us airborne and to lead us directly to some of the most profound discussions of the conference.

As regards the rest, the controversial rest, I have not observed in any of the contributions what I expected I might find: that is to say, any defense of inflation per se. I only noted that Professor Blackhurst at one stage made some reference to the absence of discussion of a tolerable rate of inflation, and I thought—perhaps I misunderstood him—that he was suggesting that I was rather dodging the issue by making the comparison between the bearable rate of, say, 2 percent, and the rates achieved in hyperinflation.

Well, I daresay I gave that impression, though it was not my intention. My eyes were fixed quite firmly on what is happening at home in the United Kingdom at this moment, where the value of money is deteriorating at quite a brisk pace. Prices are officially said to have risen in the last twelve months by over 8 percent, and I should be very surprised indeed if in the next twelve months they don't rise by at least 10 percent. It is that sort of process—Heaven grant that it be not speeded up still further—that I had in mind in the slightly disparaging remarks which I made about the inflationary process.

So much for conceptions and value judgments. The survey of what has been said at this conference falls quite naturally into two parts. We discussed causes, and we discussed possible cures; and although dividing things on that principle involves some unnatural surgical operations in the utterances of particular persons, I think on balance that it is the best classification to adopt.

As regards causes, I think we all would agree with the conception of inflation as an excess of actual or anticipated expenditure over supply at constant prices—a process which brings about an adjustment of prices in order to achieve some aggregate equalization. The question is, how does it arise? And here, I think, implicit in all our discussion has been a distinction between initiating causes and general conditions. Now, so far as initiating causes are concerned, I see no reason to depart from the classification which has become habitual in recent years—namely, causes operating on the demand side and causes operating on the cost side. I agree with Fritz Machlup that the division is to some extent artificial, and that within the two limiting cases of aggressive cost inflation and pure demand inflation is a range of intermediate cases where it is hard to say which is the chicken and which is the egg. But for purposes of this discussion, I think this crude division is quite helpful.

Not so much has been said explicitly about demand inflation as about the other kind—chiefly, I suppose, because it is all rather old hat so far as sophisticated economists are concerned. We should all agree—Bob Mundell, I hope, would agree—that demand inflation can arise from excessive government expenditure or, putting the same thing in another way, from an inflationary deficit. That's tautology. Or it can arise because of a change in profit prospects to which the structure of interest rates has not made a sufficient adjustment. In this connection, Bob's example of a change in the marginal productivity of investment because of a change in the nature of communications is an extraordinarily stimulating one. I am not clear that we devoted as much attention to this particular set of possibilities as its importance deserves. I think that when we come to read Randall Hinshaw's book on what we've been saying, we may feel that perhaps a session might have been devoted to the discussion of the international interest-rate structure and the effect that it has had in transmitting various sorts of aggregate movements.

Perhaps it is an old-fashioned view, but I am myself quite sure that the interest-rate structure is important in the causation of these aggregate movements. Businessmen appear before government committees, beat their breasts, and swear that the rate of interest doesn't mean a thing to them, but as soon as the rate of interest is raised in some attempt to control the situation, you find them all giving interviews to financial journalists, saying what an

unfortunate thing it is and how they hope that cheap money will
be restored again. I am quite clear that the interest structure is not,
as some people would sometimes persuade themselves, a sort of
ancient monument which is interesting, which perhaps is useful to
college bursars, but which has no great relevance to the contemporary situation. I don't think that we should be deterred from
believing that interest rates have a considerable potential effect.

Interest rates in recent time—money interest rates—have been on
the high side. That, of course, is a mild way of putting it; interest
rates have seldom been so high in the Western world. But here the
distinction between the money rate and the real rate of interest is
quite fundamentally important. While I wouldn't venture to gen-
eralize for countries other than my own, I am quite clear that, so
far as the United Kingdom is concerned, real interest rates are still
very low; and there certainly are some suckers about who are lending to the British government at the present time at negative real
rates of interest. At any rate, my summing up of what I believe to
be the implicit point of view of various contributors to this conference is that we should not dismiss the possibility of demand inflation and that, in fact, there has been quite a lot of demand inflation
knocking about in the last two decades.

But now, a stern voice from my right—my dear friend, Roy
Harrod, whom I have known longer than any of you except
Gottfried—called us to order, and said that cost inflation is the
order of the day. He pointed out in ringing tones that cost inflation is the novelty, the dominating novelty which, in a true perspective, overshadows the whole situation. He went on to suggest
that to explain it, let alone cure it, we should need a conference
composed somewhat differently from this—one in which there was
an adequate infusion of sociologists; or, rather, since I believe he
has certain reservations about professional sociologists, a selection
of people, whom Roy would himself pick out, who might be relied
upon to make significant sociological observations. And then,
although there were some differences of opinion among members
of the conference on how this fact of cost inflation was to be interpreted, and perhaps on how it was to be cured, very significant
figures were contributed by Mr. McClellan concerning the way in
which cost inflation has been manifesting itself in certain parts of
the American economy.

Let me say at once, in pursuing my unswerving task of seeking to eliminate causes of friction and disagreement where they are capable of elimination, that I completely agree with Sir Roy.
I can't understand why he said that he disagreed with that part of my opening address. I think he was reading into it perhaps certain overtones of policy on which it is conceivable that we should disagree a little. But of course I agree about the prevalence of cost inflation in certain parts of the world; and this isn't a new point of view. The first essay I published when Sir Roy and I were both released from government service after the war was a long review of Beveridge's *Full Employment in a Free Society*, in which I discussed at considerable length the possible emergence of cost inflation under the Beveridgean prescriptions. Be that as it may, I have no doubt at all that, at the present time, the United Kingdom presents a picture of a pure Machlupian type of aggressive cost inflation. Day by day, if you open the *Financial Times* or any well-informed London newspaper, you will find information relating to wage demands, the like of which have never taken place before, so far as I know, in the history of the country or perhaps even in the history of the world—calm demands for an increase of, say, 35 percent in wage rates at a time when the proportion of profits in the GNP, never more than about 14 percent, has been reduced by this pressure to something below 10 percent. In my hybrid capacity up to recently as half economist and half entrepreneur, I have been absolutely up to the neck in this sort of thing.

The problem is how to explain it. On this matter, Sir Roy seems to me to be becoming just a bit mystical. I know he isn't mystical fundamentally—he is one of the most reasonable persons in my acquaintance—but he invoked student unrest, the spread of crime and violence, the general instability of the world: positively an apocalyptic vision of something which has happened to this part of the universe.

And I don't altogether disagree. We are talking about something which is rather new, and we do need to look at it from all points of view—not merely from our narrow view as more or less orthodox economists. It may be that there are some sociological considerations of a pretty broad and banal type which go some way toward explaining some parts of this manifestation.

Thus I personally have no doubt at all, speaking for my own country, that there has been a certain deterioration in the quality of trade-union leadership. In my young days, when I was sowing my wild oats as a member of the labor movement and as secretary to a prominent Labour party politician, I used to meet the great trade-union leaders of the 1920s. Well, some of them at least were chaps who, if they were living in the welfare state, would have been picked out of the elementary schools, given a good education, passed on to the universities and then into the ranks of top management or, perhaps, academic life. Anyway, they wouldn't have been where they were, and I have the feeling that, nowadays, the people who are entering into labor negotiations, with one or two distinguished exceptions, are far less impressive individuals.

Well, that's a sociological explanation of a disposition to rather less reason than prevailed in the past. And it may be that there are other explanations of this kind. Certainly, student unrest, where it is not due to the behavior of a handful of pathological revolutionaries, can be partly explained as the anxiety of the volatile and sensitive young concerning the uncertainty of the world, the general sense of the falling away of standards, and so on. It may be that, in the long perspective of history, Sir Roy's vision may be vindicated, and it will be said that the earth was passing through a belt of laughing gas or poisonous gas and that for the time being we all went mad.

But I have an alternative explanation which I want to put to him, because it's not altogether incompatible with his view. It may be that in the sociological bloodstream, so to speak, there are all the time circulating certain poisonous viruses which in many states of society are quiescent and only come to life when the outside temperature reaches a certain level, or when certain expectations prevail about the behavior of one's fellows. I suspect that this kind of explanation goes quite a long way to account for what has been happening in the United Kingdom.

And here I am speaking very seriously. If you look at our history over the last twenty years or so, it is, from one point of view, an economic history which has been under the shadow of balance-of-payments difficulties. And although I don't believe for a moment that the average member of the working class knows much about the balance of payments or the difficulties to which it gives rise, it certainly is true that, in the upper reaches of politics, and among Labour members of Parliament and the trade unionists with whom they consort, apprehension concerning the balance of payments has been a pretty strong restraining influence on the disposition to take advantage of current ideology with regard to the volume of employment.

Now it so happens that, because of the 1967 devaluation and after suitable hints from Marcus Fleming's myrmidons speeding across the Atlantic at quarterly intervals to see that treasury officials are behaving properly, the balance of payments has swung into quite an agreeable position, with a comfortable surplus—very much pro tem. Unfortunately, some Labour politicians, disappointed and frustrated at the effect of the June elections, and wishing to keep up their spirits, boast of the surplus which their wise policy brought into being, congratulate their opposite numbers on the treasury bench on the fortunate situation that they've inherited, and throw out hints that, because of this, it is possible to do everything the heart could desire in the way of social policy and all the things that they themselves have been frustrated from doing for so many years. I suspect that this is part of the sociological background which Sir Roy had in mind; no government in the United Kingdom—and I imagine that this holds throughout the democracies of the world—no government is prepared to allow unemployment to grow indefinitely, so why hold back on excessive wage demands? After all, inflation doesn't hurt you if you get in first!

In this connection, let me say a word on the Phillips curve, about which Bob Mundell made such disparaging remarks. My view of the matter is somewhat different. I have always found it one of the great statistical puzzles why, with such changing institutions in the U.K. background, the curve should work so well decade after decade, with occasional exceptions which ingenuity could easily explain. It has seemed to me that there was nothing rational behind the constancy of the Phillips curve; it just was, so to speak, one of those empirical mysteries that no one had yet succeeded in finding an explanation for. On the other hand, believing as one does that there is a certain amount of continuity in the world, I do wonder whether the curve has become quite so discredited as Bob was say-

ing; and I was slightly reassured when Marcus Fleming made one
or two suggestions that perhaps, after all, it hadn't completely
collapsed.

It is true that, in the United Kingdom, the curve appears to
have shifted somewhat. In the past, the point at which inflationary
tendencies commenced in the price level was around 2.3 – 2.5 percent unemployment, and now the percentage is a little over 3, is it
not? Well, it is not difficult to think of institutional changes which
account for that. In the last few years, acts of social legislation
have been passed in the United Kingdom which make it really far
less urgent a matter for a man to look for a job. The provisions
which now obtain regarding redundancy payments create a situation which is really skies apart from the situation which prevailed
even in the early 1960s, and one wouldn't therefore find it at all
surprising that, whatever the forces which lie behind the Phillips
generalization, they have not come very powerfully into operation
at an unemployment rate of under 3 percent.

But that is all very speculative, and I must pass on. What I do
say—and here I hope I don't really disagree with Sir Roy—is that,
whatever these sociological forces are, they can only manifest
themselves if there is a certain degree of elasticity in the monetary
system. I am sure that they couldn't operate for long with an absolutely fixed money supply, however that is defined. And I don't
think they could operate for very long if we had a money supply
which was advancing at a moderate sort of speed of, roughly
speaking, little more than the advance of GNP. Surely, the cases
in human history when the velocity of circulation has shown an
almost indefinite disposition to increase have been cases of hyperinflation, when expectations have prevailed that the money system
would be abandoned and a new money substituted. Outside the
cases of hyperinflation, I think that there is a sort of limit to the
increase in velocity of circulation, provided that the money supply
is not expected also to increase pretty briskly.

This brings me to the part of our discussion dealing with the
general conditions which have permitted the increases of aggregate
expenditure, whether from the demand side or from the cost side.
And here, surely, we should all agree that we had some of the most
entertaining and profound episodes of the conference. I can't say
how much I have learned, for example, from the analysis which has

been made by various contributors to the discussion of the more intimate details of the behavior of the Eurodollar market.

To try to deal with this matter in some sort of logical sequence, let me refer first to our discussion of the U.S. payments deficit. There was not as much discussion of this subject as, coming from the outside, I should have expected. We didn't analyze very profoundly the causes of the U.S. deficit. Instead, we focused attention on the deficiencies of the gold-exchange standard, or, as I in present circumstances prefer to call it, the dollar-exchange standard—in particular, the effects on money supply in general of the habit which has grown up among central banks of holding dollars as part of their reserves.

And at this point, I must turn aside just to note the very important pronouncements made by Monsieur Rueff, who surely we all agree has done so much to clarify thought on this matter, even if we have not always agreed with him on remedies. I must draw attention to his positive declaration that he has never regarded the United States as the initial culprit in this process of degeneration—that the blame must be laid fairly and squarely with the creditor nations which adopted this unfortunate habit—although it seems that the thought had passed through his mind, from time to time, that perhaps the United States had in the end rather benefited from the arrangement!

Then we passed on to the elaborate intricacies of the Eurodollar market. There was a certain amount of disagreement about the genesis of the market. Gottfried Haberler argued strongly that the market would not have arisen in its present form if it had not been for Regulation Q and all shorts of mysterious formal and informal capital controls which I personally have never been able to understand and which I have always mentally condemned a little when I've read about them in Gottfried's writing; he certainly makes a very strong case for the view that they ought not to have come into being. Others felt that the controls were only part of the story. Our main discussion was about the significance of what I call the Machlup demonstration—what Bob Mundell summarized in an imperishable phrase: the tendency, through this market apparatus, for "low-powered" money to become "high-powered" money. And we had a good deal of talk on the significance in the modern world, with all its tight controls and its aspirations for cut-and-dried visions

of the future, of the floating about of all this stateless money—
uncontrolled and, perhaps, not easily controllable.

I ventured from my sort of village-idiot standpoint to ask
where the lender of last resort, if any, is in the Eurodollar market.
Various answers were put forward from different sides of the table
—some reasurring, some not. Walter Salant tried to assure us that
in the end, perhaps, we could rely on the Fed. Eric Roll, who lives,
moves, and has his being in the Eurodollar market, hinted that
there were possibilities, not of impending doom or anything of that
sort, but of serious trouble if there were certain kinds of break-
down. I think most of us agreed that the Eurodollar mechanism
serves a positive purpose in restoring life and mobility to the international capital market, but I think most of us also felt that the
present situation could not be regarded as altogether satisfactory.
We noted the remarkable growth of the volume of business in this
area—not so surprising if one takes account of the Machlup demonstration and possible multiplier effects. And one could not see—at
least I could not see—any evidence of a curb to that growth except
where it was the result of some deliberate policy.

So much for a broad summary of our discussion about causes.
And now about cures. Apparently, we all want to cure inflation;
there is no representative—at least no articulate representative—of
the pro-inflation school present. No one raised any disagreement
with the proposition which I advanced in my opening remarks that
it is possible, given sufficient resolution and flexibility of mind,
for a country to opt out of world inflation by appreciation of the
exchange rate or by judicious management of a float. Contrary to
my expectation, no one objected that there were possible grave
political difficulties connected with that particular approach, difficulties which had been illustrated in recent history. I was rather
surprised that Gardner Patterson, who made a valuable statement
on the subject of commercial policy, did not expatiate at any
length on the difficulties that would arise for him as a GATT official if there were much tendency to opt out of the world's inflation by means of continually shifting important exchange rates.

All that was not discussed, but there was considerable discussion
of another approach—namely, incomes policy. Roy, you reproached
me for not talking about incomes policy in my opening address.
Eric reproached me, too, though he was not frightfully upset: he

made it clear that it was not the woman he really loves; still, he had had something to do with her, and he would have liked my opinion of what the girl was like while he was walking out with her. Well, this omission was absolutely deliberate, because I couldn't help thinking that some reproach of that sort would arise and would give me something to talk about in this last meeting when I should have you all at my mercy. I have, in fact, spoken about incomes policy recently, and made some slight concession, my dear Roy, to your position, although probably not nearly as much as you would wish.

Let me expatiate a little on the problems of incomes policy as I see them. There are two leading types that we should consider; there is the overall freeze of prices and wages (or prices alone or wages alone), and there is incomes policy in the sense of an attempt, by voluntary means or otherwise, to regulate the general level and relationships of incomes, particularly wages.

Now do let me make this clear. I have been awfully doctrinaire at various times in my life. But I am not so doctrinaire as to rule out any possibility of incomes policy in an emergency, such as war or hyperinflation, and I do not rule out the possibility of the United Kingdom having to resort to this sort of thing as shock tactics in the near future; I have actually said so recently in public. My trouble is that, not being frightfully fixed on any sort of dogmas as the end of life approaches, I really don't see this thing working *à la longue*. I am really very pessimistic about the possibility of solving the overall stability problem through tactics of this sort, valuable as they conceivably can be in certain emergencies for a short time.

Let me try to make clear why I am of this frame of mind. Take freezes first. We all know what happens to price freezes in regimes of inflation. Demand exceeds supply, goods become scarce in the shops, and you get the disturbing phenomenon of distribution according to queue rather than distribution according to the purse. It is not clear to anybody, I should have thought, that distribution according to the time that you have to line up in the shops is a juster way of distributing commodities than distribution by price.

Much worse than that is the fact that in a very short time—and this is awfully down to earth—it makes rogues of us all. If you were in the manufacturing business, Roy, and the prices of your products were fixed, what you would do—unless you were the entrepreneur of that very unreal ideal type, the single-product firm—would be to shift your productive arrangements just a little, and turn out products which weren't in the price schedule, or you would slightly lower the quality while retaining the name. I won't say you would do this if you were in business of your own; but if you were representing the shareholders, you would feel, "Well, my duty is to see that we don't go into the red with these increased costs." This is not just textbook fantasy, it does happen: I assure you it happens. You only have to go a very little way into business to hear the discussion of possible tactics in the case of a freeze to realize that these things can and do take place.

A similar insidious process can take place where the fixation of incomes is concerned. Let me take a case I know something about. Suppose, Roy, you were a newspaper proprietor, and one of your chaps turned up one morning, saying, "Lord X has offered me 500 pounds a year more than you're paying me." What would you say to him? Well, you might say, "All right, let Lord X have you. We don't like you all that much—and good luck!" But suppose you did like him very much, and there was this ruling from your prices and incomes board that wages cannot be increased for the time being. What would you do? (For any of you who are getting suspicious, I might say that this has not actually happened in my experience; but I've thought it out, you see.) My guess is that you would scratch your head a bit and say, "Well, my boy, you know we can't do anything under this ruling while you remain what you are. But I've been thinking for some time that we needed someone with a slightly different job description; and if you are willing to take that job, which is not on our schedule at the moment, I think perhaps we might be able to pay you as much as Lord X is offering you!"

Now don't tell me that this is a fantastic example; I assure you that this is something which was going on all the time in the United Kingdom during the existence of the prices and incomes board. And it goes on at a greater rate as it becomes general because, what originally was something which might upset one's conscience a little, eventually becomes the general rule. Then, of course, if the freeze breaks down, the price increases and the wage demands that are made in order to catch up with the time that has been lost are sometimes greater than what might have happened if there had been no freeze—not always, but sometimes.

Coming to incomes policy proper, Roy, I thought you were a bit misleading about our U.K. experience shortly after the war. The Cripps measures, which I agree with you were pretty successful, were more in the nature of a freeze than of a systematic incomes policy. And they did come to an end. Aubrey Jones, who was head of our incomes and prices board, claimed once that he had been able to restrain the rise in the price level to 1 percent per annum—which isn't a frightfully spectacular achievement, although every bit helps. Well, I don't say that one shouldn't try again in certain circumstances; I don't say the thing is inconceivable in certain kinds of societies, because we have seen wage controls operating in smaller communities for some time—although, strangely enough, most of them seem to have broken down just recently. But I do say that I think you tremendously underestimate the administrative difficulties. I know that in many connections trade-union leaders are apt to be reasonable and nice people. But arguing with them across the table is rather different.

And here, Roy, I must invoke a little sociology against you. The relativity problem in a society which is not organized on a totalitarian basis is overwhelmingly difficult. Your trade-union secretary is *paid* in order to preserve relativities; and we all know how fantastically intractable trade unions can be as regards demarcation disputes. The relativity problem is incredibly difficult when you are trying to administer an economy the size of the United Kingdom, with its fragmentation of trade unions, even if you are dealing with the larger industrial unions. Moreover, on top of that, Roy, you mentioned quite rightly that the trade unions will demand a limitation of dividends; you, yourself, suggested that perhaps you might agree to a surtax on dividends. But, in a situation in which you really want investment to be gingered up—in a situation like that of the United Kingdom, where surely one of the main reasons for the lamentably poor rate of growth has been inadequate investment—the limitation of dividends is something which one can only propose as shock tactics; one does not want it in season and out of season.

Thus, in the end, I do believe that the *permanent* stabilization of aggregate demand by incomes policy involves a degree of control, not only of rates and earnings and side benefits, but even in the last analysis of conditions of entry which would do a lot to turn our society into something very, very different from what it is at the moment and something which certainly would be resisted hotly by the best and most reasonable elements in the trade-union movement. Do remember, Roy, that when you and I were involved as economic advisers in trying to keep the war economy on an even keel, the greatest of all our trade-union leaders in this century, Ernest Bevin, who certainly was enormously successful as Minister of Labor, never dared to control wages directly.

Let me come back to my own position. My view is that, whatever we do as shock tactics in an emergency, the optimal solution in a free society is to persuade the various parties to collective bargaining that the government is not prepared to provide more finance than will permit incomes advancing with productivity, or, just to make a small concession to human nature, a *little* bit more than productivity, but not much more. I don't say that you can bring this about all at once. The cruel position in the United Kingdom is that if one were at once to apply the braking mechanism according to the optimal norms, one would certainly bring about a colossal economic disaster. The thing must be done slowly and with recourse to all sorts of perhaps rather dubious interim expedients. But, in the end, my utopia lies much more in that spread of understanding and good sense than in more control from the center.

This brings me now back to aggregate expenditure and to what I will call the "Bob Mundell difficulty." I would have thought that in recent years, rightly or wrongly, economists would have acquired the habit of regarding monetary and fiscal controls of aggregate expenditure, not as mutually antagonistic instruments, but rather as complementary and as capable, at any rate, of working in the same direction. This, I think, lay behind Gottfried Haberler's adverse reaction to Bob; and certainly in my thinking about regaining control of the U.K. economy, I have always thought of monetary policy, which I thoroughly support, as being to some extent complemented by the judicious use of that admirable fiscal invention, the "regulator," whereby the chancellor of the exchequer, without introducing a new budget, can alter the rate of indirect taxation up and down within due limits. I don't know whether Marcus Fleming invented it, but it came from that stable.

I am not sure that Bob says no to this. But Bob—here I lay down a sociological law—is seldom wrong. And even when you disagree with him, you must disagree with your hat in the hand. Bob's case is that there is a qualitative difference between the two instruments, and that taxation affects not only aggregate demand but aggregate supply. With his eyes fully glued on the contemporary U.S. situation, he is led to conceive of a state of affairs in which the money control can be tightened up, with immensely beneficial effects on the rate of increase of prices, and in which the tax burden is lightened, with beneficial effects on the volume of production, so that, again, the tendency to a fall in the value of money is mitigated.

Well, after a night of sighs, I see his point, but I wonder whether Bob would accept these glosses on his position. First of all, to get the Mundell effect, does it not depend on the type of tax change? I certainly can think of some frightfully iniquitous kinds of taxation which have been holding down investment being removed, and the effect of that removal on supply being so much greater than the effect on the disposition to spend on consumption that the net effect might be very beneficial in the Mundell sense. Therefore I wonder whether he would agree, too, that the criterion of applicability of his prescription must be judged in the end on a twofold basis; it must be judged not only by his supply effect but also on the effect on aggregate expenditure. I am not sure, you see, that the thing always works in one way. I think, for instance, of the example that I put earlier to Bob: that, for some reason or other, a war is being conducted old-style—1914 style—with much too little taxation and much too much manufacture of money. And I ask him if he would agree that in those circumstances, with the system more or less fully employed, the substitution of properly increased taxation would have a beneficial effect in restraining inflation.

I don't want to be too provocative to a man who is chained to silence; I've abused my position already in that respect in regard to

Sir Roy. If Bob can induce President Nixon to change his present policy in the Mundell direction, I shall watch with fascinated and detached interest the result. But when he was talking, I couldn't help feeling—and doubtless this was weakness of the flesh, Bob, you must not despise me for that—that I did not want our chancellor of the exchequer to be aware of these views, because I am not sure that he would go all the way with you. He might be inclined to say, "Oh, money, you know, that's an unimportant thing; the thing that really matters is what happens on the tax side." I feel that Bob would give the chancellor rather too much encouragement toward fiscal leniency. But perhaps I am wrong.

Coming back to credit and credit control, I think we have all agreed that the international situation is far from satisfactory and that the position as regards official foreign-exchange reserves and the Eurodollar market gives rise, if not to apprehension of an impending doom, at any rate to feelings that all is not well in the capacity to bring conscious control to bear on the stabilization of the world situation. Fritz Machlup made a plea that we can all agree with—that there should be more knowledge about all this, that there should be more statistics supplied by central banks. Well, that's OK; it's nice to find something about which we can be unanimous. Then various members of the conference advanced various plans for the elimination of the offset arrangements—various improvements of the dollar-exchange standard. Machlup enumerated some, Robert Triffin called for a ceiling on official currency holdings, and Monsieur Rueff of course went even further. And at one point, Gottfried Haberler chimed in and said to Fritz Machlup, "You're going back to gold!"

Well, this provokes me to a slight terminological excursus. The gold standard has a double aspect which we have to keep in mind in framing suitable semantics. First, it has the aspect of procuring an automatic adjustment of international economic relations. If there is no compensation for emerging deficits, if there is no sterilization at the other end—in other words, if there are only the automatic compensatory movements that you would have in a closed economy, then you have an automatic adjustment mechanism of a type which used to be claimed for the gold standard—and I have no doubt that, from time to time, the gold standard operated that way. I would only point out that the same arrangements would be possible with an international dollar standard if the Eurodollar market were to disappear and all offsetting were to be eliminated.

But there is a second aspect; and I think that before you call a standard a gold standard, this additional requirement also has to be fulfilled—namely, that the ultimate supply of credit throughout the area where this standard prevails depends upon the volume of gold forthcoming from the mines, minus what goes into industrial uses. And that was what I had in mind, Monsieur Rueff, when I said that I didn't think we were likely to go back to gold. I don't think that we are within a thousand miles of a gold standard of that kind now, nor have been for a very long time, because surely the fact is that it's what the central banks decide nowadays on reserve ratios, and so on, that determines the ultimate volume of credit—far, far more than what happens through chemical extraction of gold from various parts of the earth's surface.

This leads me back to the position of the dollar in the present world. Personally, I rather agree with Monsieur Rueff that the position of the dollar is not such as to leave one with a clear vision of a cloudless future. I can see clouds the size of a man's hand on the horizon which might boil up into quite severe trouble again. The present arrangements as regards demands on gold reserves, for example, are awfully fragile, and no doubt they depend upon the plighted word of extremely honorable men, meeting in masks and disguises at various fashionable places. But I can conceive of the world splitting up into two blocs, a dollar bloc and a European currency bloc—a situation which some of you might regard as optimal. I wouldn't say that such a system was at all unmanageable; there might be a floating rate of exchange between these two gigantic systems, and we might jog along in a way which was congenial to many of you who have had love affairs with the idea of floating rates in a rather less orderly world than that.

But apart from this option—and now I approach the end of these too long remarks—what are the possibilities of change within the present system? Bob Mundell reproached me for being a bit skeptical about the IMF, and perhaps I am wrong there. I am all in harmony with Bob's suggestion of some Atlantic committee, perhaps under the auspices of the IMF, to discuss the dollar problem and the influence which the Federal Reserve has upon credit conditions throughout the world. Perhaps at a later stage, Marcus Fleming could be induced to talk just a little bit about that.

Finally, I come to that splendid statement by John Parke Young, bringing with it the refreshing breath of the days when we collaborated together at the Bretton Woods conference—his bold suggestion for the initiation of discussions to create an international currency. Well, I am all for that. But I am sure Mr. Young would agree with me that we are at once plunged into a sea of politics here and that the political considerations are by no means conducive to optimism.

I ask first the question: Supposing that the international currency is created, to what extent will people be allowed to use it once the finance ministers become alive to the fact that people want to use it? To my way of thinking, one of the most important things in the monetary history of the twentieth century is the invalidation of the gold clause in commercial contracts at the beginning of the 1930s. If it had not been invalidated by the various high courts of justice, of course we should all have switched over pretty soon to making our contracts in terms of gold; and history since 1930 would have been very different, for better or worse. My own suspicion is that finance ministers would not like us to go very far in using the international currency as long as they retain complete sovereignty in their respective areas. There would be various limitations; you could use it for this and use it for that, but it would not be a truly universal thing until there had been all sorts of political adjustments.

But a more fundamental question worries and nags me when I think of the future of the world for my grandchildren and for future generations. When I think of the present chaos of the Western world vis-à-vis the totalitarian menaces, when I cast my mind back for analogies, I think of the glorious civilization of the Greek city states, none of whose leaders had sufficient vision to consolidate a political system which would have saved them from the impact of greater, less scrupulous, less civilized powers. I ask myself, will decent, conscientious finance ministers be prepared to abrogate sufficiently their powers over the creation of money by their local central banks, which the creation of a truly international currency would involve? Unless there are political guarantees as regards defense and as regards solidarity in foreign policy, will they be prepared to surrender their sovereignty until the Western world has shown more disposition to political solidarity than it does at the present time?

There is a ray of hope, perhaps, in the movement toward integration in continental Europe; it may be that this movement will be reinforced by the accession of the United Kingdom. But while I go all the way with Mr. Young in longing for the creation of a unit of account and a medium of exchange which has at least Western cosmopolitan significance, and which does not give rise to all the arts and strategems and confusions and ignominies of the last forty or fifty years, I come back to the old point which many of you have heard me make at other get-togethers and conferences— that, in the last analysis, the solution of the monetary problem, the solution of the problem of international inflation, is a political rather than an economic problem.

Chairman THORP: I do not feel that it's appropriate for me to make a light-hearted remark at this moment, when I am filled with wonder at the skill with which Lord Robbins has performed his very difficult assignment. I know that we are all very grateful for his remarks and for the contributions which he would have made from time to time during the conference if the chairman had permitted him to do so.

Two of the members whose names were most often mentioned in Lord Robbins's summary have asked if they could have a very few minutes to discuss that summary. As a matter of personal privilege, I shall give them the floor, but shall be quite demanding that they confine their remarks to not more than six minutes or so. First, I shall turn the floor over to Sir Roy.

Sir ROY HARROD: Thank you very much; I will be brief. Lionel did refer to me more than once during his discourse, and there are one or two points which I would like to make clear.

One is a negative point. According to my study, we have had a very restrained money policy in the United Kingdom. I have investigated the matter in various ways. In my opinion, one should leave out currency notes. These are purely passive; their issue will be in proportion—not exactly, but fairly closely—to the money value of the national income. As regards bank deposits, time deposits are very prominent both in our statistics and in U.S. statistics; the question is whether to include them in our definition of

money. The ordinary money supply, as commonly defined, does
not include time deposits. If you omit time deposits in the case of
the United Kingdom, you will find that, apart from occasional
aberrations, demand deposits have risen only very slightly more
than real national income, and much less than money income. If
you take demand deposits as your criterion, the velocity of circulation has been rising on and off, not for just a couple of years, but
over the last twenty years. It has simply gone up and up.

You may say that there has been some simple explanation, such
as the introduction of credit cards, for example. Maybe, but on the
face of it, it looks as if we have had a steadily rising velocity of
circulation at a time when the increase in the supply of money
has been very restrained.

Now if you add in time deposits, you get a greater increase in
the money supply, but still one which is way below the increase in
the money value of the national income. That is my negative point.
It's going to encourage our resolution to face up to what has to be
faced if we lose our faith that, if only we could deal with the
money supply better, things would work out and the inflation
would go away. If we apprehend that the increase in the money
supply has been very moderate and restrained, and has been far
below the increase in the money value of the national income, we
will begin to look for a different solution. Also, of course, in the
United Kingdom we have had a tremendously deflationary fiscal
policy, with huge budget surpluses, and in the most recent period
all the capital expenditures undertaken by the British government
have been paid for out of taxes. That is not what people thought
would happen when they voted the nationalization of industries
some years ago.

Now to the positive point—on incomes policy. If you dislike inflation as much as both Lionel and I dislike it, then you've got to
face up to the idea of an incomes policy. I have never claimed that
such a policy would be easy; it is a major operation and not like
the push-button operation of simply selling securities in the market
in order to reduce the money supply.

I agree that a freeze is simply a shock tactic, and I would only
propose it for a limited period. One wants the freeze in order to
get the round-table going, to thrash out among those who are responsible the various ingredients in incomes policy. While I would

never think that there could be anything like a permanent freeze on consumer prices, I would say that there ought to be a permanent policy of a ceiling on wage increases. I would not place direct limits on profits or dividends; for obvious reasons, you want a lot of profit to encourage and finance new investment. My proposal would be to have an across-the-board tax on dividends in order to insure that the overall average of dividends (plus bonus shares and all that sort of thing) was not rising at a greater rate than employee income.

Chairman THORP: Thank you very much. I have a suspicion that Bob Mundell is studying the supply of money with a gentleman upstairs; since he is not here, we will reserve a moment for him a bit later and turn now to Jacques Rueff.

JACQUES RUEFF: After this admirable address by Lord Robbins, I hesitate to lower the level of our discussion by the modest remarks I have to present. In any case, I shall be brief.

Lord Robbins says that he does not want what he calls a "return to gold," because he does not want a regime in which the aggregate quantity of money depends on the fortuitous production of gold. I think that I would myself be against such a regime if I felt that the volume of credit was exclusively determined by the volume of monetary gold. But that is a complicated matter of monetary theory; I only want to raise the point.

Several people around this table have said that they agree with my diagnosis but not with my prescription. I feel very grateful to Fritz Machlup, who has gone very far in my direction by proposing an international agreement under which central banks would no longer place their dollars anywhere except in a blocked account with the Federal Reserve. But I think there is little hope that such an agreement will be possible. What I have in mind is also an international agreement, but on a quite different basis; it is an international convention under which countries would agree to a regime in which central banks do not count foreign exchange as international monetary reserves. Of course, central banks would be permitted to have foreign exchange for their current needs, but they would not be permitted to issue money, as they do now, against foreign exchange.

If this idea were accepted, it would mean that a deficit in the balance of payments would have to be paid in gold rather than in foreign exchange. Dollar balances would become more or less useless, since they could not be utilized to settle deficits.

This is why I have long advocated a doubling of the price of gold. Until rather recently, such a move would have made it possible for the United States and the United Kingdom to redeem in gold the outstanding official balances in dollars and sterling. But now, with the immense development of Eurodollars and other Eurocurrencies, simply doubling the price of gold would no longer solve the problem. The amount of official dollars is now much smaller than the volume of Eurodollars, and if some day this mass of Eurocurrency should unfreeze, with people demanding currencies other than dollars, the situation could become very serious.

So I don't think that the solution I advised in the past—a doubling of the price of gold—is still sufficient. I am afraid that the problem is now out of the hands of men. Events will induce central banks either to refuse to increase their dollar balances or to ask for repayment. Either situation would mean an embargo on gold from the United States and a depreciation of the dollar on the foreign-exchange markets. That would be an immense danger for the world; it might mean the loss of all liberalization, of all progress achieved since the war toward the restoration of satisfactory international economic arrangements. I still hope that we can avoid this danger but, taking account of present realities so clearly described by Lord Robbins, I am not optimistic about the prospects for achieving agreement on a rational settlement of this difficult problem.

Chairman THORP: Monsieur Rueff has added another threat to the future which I guess we all will have to recognize as being with us. Now that Bob Mundell has returned, I will give him his right of personal privilege to comment briefly on Lord Robbins's summary.

ROBERT A. MUNDELL: The first point I want to raise about Lord Robbins' closing statement concerns the matter of war finance. If one is in the unfortunate position of having to finance a war, the appropriate way to do so is through a mixture of tax finance and bond finance. I completely agree with Lord Robbins that inflationary finance would not be the correct approach; there is no disagreement whatsoever on that issue. The only question here is what one does in a situation where there is excess capacity in the economy. Where there is an extra 2 or 3 percentage points of unemployment over and above the minimum frictional and other unemployment associated with a "full" employment level, then there is room for substantial expansion in the economy as a whole. In such cases, certainly in peacetime, it is necessary to distinguish sharply between monetary policy and fiscal policy. In the United States, I have made the case for tax reduction, combined with tighter money, with the aim of moving the unemployment rate down from 6 percent to 4 percent or below. The extra $50 billion or so in aggregate supply would help greatly both in reducing unemployment and in checking inflation.

The only other point I would like to raise concerns Lord Robbins' conclusion that international monetary reform and the establishment of an international currency are political questions. I completely agree, but that does not mean that the initiative for advancing toward an improved international monetary system and toward the creation of a world currency—both of which I strongly support—cannot be undertaken by economists. International monetary reform as an instrument for dealing with the problem of world inflation is a matter on which we must continue to think as energetically and as profoundly as we can.

Chairman THORP: Thank you, Bob. We are now ready to look at the future from another perspective. One of the areas which we have underexplored in our discussion has been the role of international agencies in coping with world inflation. Accordingly, I think it is appropriate that we ask Marcus Fleming if he would take a few minutes to review the possibilities, as he sees them, of dealing with inflationary pressures by more effective use of these institutions.

J. MARCUS FLEMING: There is a view that any pretention to scientific knowledge has to be proven by the ability to make prophecies, and that is why I didn't refuse to have a look at the future—though I must confess that my own crystal ball is distinctly cloudy.

Perhaps I might say something first about the direct inflation issue before going on to the question of the reserve system. My impression, I must admit, has been that a gentle decline in the real return on capital has been taking place. Certainly, real interest rates have tended to decline. I think that with the Americanization of the economies of the industrial countries having already gone a considerable distance, and with the prospect in those countries of some decline in population growth, it seems possible that there would be a decline in the spontaneous and autonomous tendencies toward inflation in the world.

I know that Bob Mundell has cited developments in the communications industry which he thinks point to a different conclusion regarding interest rates. I am not enough of a technical expert to be able to judge that very well, but I would agree with him to the extent that I don't see any likelihood of relapsing to chronic stagnation or anything of that sort. Whatever may be happening in the communications industry, the need for complete rebuilding of cities, the continuation of the trend toward equalization of incomes, the persistence of war dangers—and long may they persist because they won't disappear until war has taken place—seem to be a sufficient guarantee against any stagnation in the future. Nevertheless, as I say, I think there is some possibility of a falling off, to some slight extent, in spontaneous demand pressures.

We were told yesterday as regards the cost-push element that monopolistic tendencies were not really increasing. This may be so; nevertheless, I would expect some continuation of the deterioration of the Phillips curve. I am not speaking of the short-term Phillips curve, which has been pushed up by inflationary anticipations, but of the longer-term Phillips curve I spoke of yesterday. I would expect that to deteriorate somewhat because of the falling off in productivity growth which is almost bound to take place in the industrial parts of the world other than the United States and, I hope, the United Kingdom. The very high rates of productivity growth have helped to keep the Phillips curve relatively low in continental Europe. I would expect that situation to worsen somewhat, so that we might have a tendency in Europe for the Phillips curve to deteriorate as it has in the United Kingdom and the United States.

If that is so, then we are up against this choice: either we have to have more price inflation, or more unemployment, or more price control. My impression is that we shall have a little bit of all of these; that is the way things have been going. I think that the establishment of a single currency in Europe—if that comes about—will accentuate the difficulties here, and may lead to a situation in which unemployment in Europe increases to about the American level. It will also be more difficult to apply incomes policies, because, as I said yesterday, these are more successfully applied in

small countries like the Scandinavian countries, Australia, New
Zealand, and the Netherlands. But I do feel that there will be strong
pressures on politicians to interfere more and more with incomes
and prices.

While I share many of the feelings of Lord Robbins on this matter, I can't help remembering, unless I greatly misread history, that
the human race has lived for much the greater part of the time
under regimes of price and wage control. And that may be the natural way for human beings to live; at any rate, I am sure that they
are not going to tolerate a system of perpetual inflation as the
price of preserving a free-market system. So we may have to bend
our effort toward getting the intervention to work on a moderately
scientific basis, by which I mean a basis that respects, in some degree, the market principle as one line of effort in trying to make
the system work a little better.

Coming to the reserve system, there has been, of course, a tremendous expansion in world reserves—about 20 percent in 1970
alone. I don't think that expansion has really had much effect on
world inflation. The present inflationary tendency obviously
started in 1968–69 when reserve growth, by general admission,
was quite inadequate. Nevertheless, honesty compels me to admit that an increase of international liquidity does have a potential influence on domestic liquidity and inflation, and that the
present inflation, though obviously not attributable to an expansion of reserves, may nevertheless have been stimulated to some
extent by an increase in international liquidity occurring in other
ways.

What I have in mind here, among other things, is the establishment of the two-tier arrangement, which enormously increased
real international liquidity in the United States; the United States
no longer feels impelled to worry about its payments deficit, even
though its reserves are no larger than before. Apart from this, the
removal of some rather marked disequilibria through the devaluation of the pound and the franc and the appreciation of the D-mark
has for the time being reduced the need for reserves and therefore
enhanced international liquidity in that way. These developments
have provided a climate of balance-of-payments ease which may
have contributed to inflationary pressure by allowing governments
to be more disposed to permit expansion than they otherwise

would have been. So I would certainly think that a continuance of reserve expansion on anything like the scale we've seen recently would be a real danger from an inflationary standpoint.

This expansion in reserves has only to a very moderate extent been the result of deliberate reserve creation in the form of special drawing rights. It has primarily resulted from an increased holding of foreign exchange in general—and the dollar in particular—resulting primarily, though not exclusively, from the U.S. payments deficit. This raises a big question in my mind—how far the maintenance of the practice of holding reserves in the form of foreign exchange is compatible with deliberate internationally controlled reserve creation. The understanding on which the SDR system was set up was that any further expansion of reserves in the form of foreign exchange would be moderate, and that if reserve centers had deficits, these would be financed largely out of their own reserves, so that world reserves would not tend to expand markedly as a result of that.

Now matters have not turned out in this way. It is here that my crystal ball becomes completely blurred. It is very difficult to ask of a reserve center that it should voluntarily finance its deficits out of its own reserves if it doesn't have to. But if the deficits are not financed from reserves, and if the deficits themselves are not checked, then we are going to get too much reserve creation.

As regards the U.S. deficit, I am really very optimistic on what one might call the basic deficit problem. If I were asked to bet, I should say that inflationary tendencies in the future will be stronger in Europe than in the United States. Thus, over time, one would expect to find the basic U.S. balance of payments improving. The question therefore arises whether in the meantime steps should be taken, perhaps along Bob Mundell's lines, which would have the result of making capital flow internationally in such a way as to bring to an end deficit-created reserves, and thus enable the SDR system—the system of international provision of reserves according to need—to continue in the manner which was originally intended.

Chairman THORP: Thank you very much. I now call on the one person whose intervention in the conference was entirely focused on the future—John Parke Young.

JOHN PARKE YOUNG: Mr. Chairman, we are faced so frequently with monetary crises and problems requiring immediate atten-

tion that we tend to neglect basic solutions. The problems which
are here and now, such as worldwide inflation, cannot be ignored;
but desirable changes in the international monetary system are too
often regarded as something for the future. They merit early action,
however, not only because of long-run benefits but because they
would materially relieve current short-run distress.

Our discussions here in Bologna on the Eurodollar, inflation,
and other current problems have been illuminating and useful. But
we need also to focus on an action program which deals with underlying causes—a program calling for changes in the international
monetary mechanism which are greatly needed and, I believe,
feasible.

The basic need is obvious; it is an international currency medium
to replace the dollar in world trade and finance. Gold has long been
inadequate as the world's currency. Sterling has had difficulties.
And now the dollar is in trouble. No national currency can perform
satisfactorily the role of an international reserve asset and a transactions currency for world trade and investment. There is a void
here which needs filling, not only for central banks but for private
business as well.

The introduction of an effectively functioning international currency is not as difficult as it might seem at first glance. As I suggested earlier at this conference, a beginning could be made fairly
simply by having the International Monetary Fund open accounts
of transferable credits for member countries. These countries would
acquire credits in the accounts by depositing gold, foreign exchange, and SDRs in large or small amounts. The transferable
credits would be acquired on a voluntary basis, and would be designed to function as gold formerly did for both public and private
transactions.

The large supply of dollars now held abroad would be convertible, at least in part, into IMF currency under regulations which
would include conversion by the United States of the dollars so
deposited into interest-bearing obligations, with maturities related
to considerations of international liquidity and of feasibility for
the United States. Other currencies deposited at the IMF would be
treated similarly. I will not go into technical aspects this morning,
but would note that the proposal goes beyond those providing

simply for the pooling of reserve assets at the International Monetary Fund, since the IMF currency would be available to the public through commercial banks, which would acquire it from their central banks.

I agree with Lord Robbins that there are political difficulties in introducing such a currency; but I would ask, what economic problem isn't confronted with serious political difficulties? And if we delay in dealing with problems because of political difficulties, where do we get?

The proposal I am making is not, I believe, as drastic a step as was the introduction of special drawing rights. Who would have thought only a few years ago that the International Monetary Fund would be allowed to create credit? Yet that is what the SDR arrangement involves. This significant development in the evolution of the world's monetary system is a long step in the direction of what I am proposing. The opening of transferable accounts would initially be less of an innovation than SDRs, although eventually—assuming the system expands—it would have far-reaching effects with substantial benefits.

The establishment of a world currency through transferable accounts at the IMF would relieve—I hesitate to say solve—so many of our problems that I feel we should not delay moving actively in this direction. Consider, for example, the critical problem of international adjustment, which is made more difficult by varying rates of inflation in different countries. A world currency would relieve this problem; to the extent that the currency were widely used, changes in exchange rates would affect fewer transactions and thus would not be such disturbing events as they are today. Under these conditions, countries would be encouraged to maintain a pattern of exchange rates more conducive to international equilibrium.

A world currency—removed from balance-of-payments and revaluation uncertainties—would tend to discourage switching from weaker into stronger currencies, and thus would tend to check the massive speculative capital flows which cause such headaches for central banks. To the extent that a world currency discouraged such capital flows while at the same time promoting international equilibrium, it would remove the basis for the maze of restrictions over trade and the flow of capital—quotas, import taxes, exchange controls, and so on—that are so frequently imposed for balance-of-payments reasons. In this and other ways, a world currency would facilitate a liberal multilateral trading system.

Such an arrangement would provide not only central banks but also private business, concerned over devaluation risks, with a stable currency in which it could have confidence. Balance sheets frequently have an item labelled "loss from currency devaluations." These losses total many millions of dollars, but measure only a small portion of the real loss from the lack of a stable world currency. The spectacular growth of multinational corporations and other world trading units makes a strong case for the availability of such a currency for private as well as for official institutions.

Finally, through such a currency, we would begin to get rid of the problems created by the dollar standard—problems so well described a few minutes ago by Marcus Fleming. The quantity of world currency would no longer be determined by the payments deficits of any country. Of course, this would mean that the United States no longer could finance its deficits by pouring dollars on the world market. But this unique privilege has few defenders, and is the source of bitter resentment against the United States. The dollar standard has in many ways become a liability to the United States. Sooner or later, it will doubtless go, although development of a satisfactory substitute will be a slow process.

Then there is the matter of a European currency bloc. Plans for European currency integration and, eventually, a European currency are well under way. Exchange-rate adjustments between such a bloc (which presumably will include sterling) and the dollar bloc may present serious problems. Debate over the rate could drag on, and in the meantime there might be long periods of disequilibrium between the two blocs and a trend toward protectionism. If we had a world currency, the problem would be less serious, and some of the political difficulties associated with rate adjustments would disappear.

The world currency I have suggested in the form of IMF transferable credits should not be convertible into gold. It would have all the international monetary functions of gold, and would be essentially "as good as gold." But looking at the matter from a practical standpoint, I don't see how it could be redeemable into gold without involving all the problems the dollar has had with gold convertibility.

Such a currency should be initiated on a voluntary basis in order to expedite its establishment. The IMF would invite members to put some of their gold, dollars, sterling, and SDRs into transferable accounts. The system could begin gradually with a few countries, but would doubtless expand as other countries saw the advantages and no longer wished to be left out. So that it could have access to the currency, private business could be expected to put pressure on governments to participate.

To the extent that the currency was used domestically—for example, in order to escape local-currency uncertainties—there could be internal problems for finance ministers, since there might be a conflict between international and domestic objectives. But as I said earlier, we should not shy away from a logical approach to our difficulties because we see certain problems. I am sure that finance ministers and central bankers are ingenious enough to find ways of dealing with them.

The International Monetary Fund is the logical agency to embark upon this project. The matter should be considered at a high level. To get recommendations in a form for amendments to the IMF Articles of Agreement and then to get action could be a matter of several years. But if we don't start, we are delaying a solution to urgent problems.

Sooner or later, something of this kind has got to come; I don't see any satisfactory alternative. As each became inadequate, the world has moved since the nineteenth century from gold, then to sterling, and then to the dollar. We are now ready for another evolutionary move to a currency adapted to the modern shrinking world, and we would do well to expedite this move as much as possible.

At Bretton Woods, the delegations were willing to undertake a bold innovation. It has worked out well. The Fund and the World Bank are examples of what can happen when we are not afraid of doing what is needed. The fact that there are political difficulties is all the more reason why we should proceed promptly. Our goal of a functioning currency cannot be reached overnight, and the time has come to take a first step.

NAME INDEX

Arndt, Sven W., 118

Bagehot, Walter, 122
Bernstein, Edward M., 63
Beveridge, Sir William, 132
Bevin, Ernest, 141
Blackhurst, Richard, 70-71, 129
Bloomfield, Arthur I., 66-67
Burgess, W. Randolph, 11
Burns, Arthur F., 89, 121

Carli, Guido, 87, 90
Collery, Arnold, 102-3, 108
Cripps, Sir Stafford, 140

De Cecco, Marcello, 84-85, 110-11
de Gaulle, Charles, 57
Disraeli, Benjamin, 97
Douglass, Gordon K., 69-70

Emminger, Otmar, 10, 32, 36, 90
Exter, John, 36, 80-81, 94-97, 111, 117, 122

Fisher, Irving, 125
Fleming, J. Marcus, 36, 82-84, 87, 106-7, 110, 123-24, 126, 142, 145, 150-51, 156
Friedman, Milton, 37, 46, 51

Haberler, Gottfried, 9, 32, 39-43, 46, 49, 69, 77-78, 80, 86, 90, 93-94, 95, 96, 113, 115-17, 118, 119, 120, 123, 131, 136, 141, 143
Haines, C. Grove, 129

Harrod, Sir Roy, 6, 9, 43-45, 46, 59, 98-99, 102-3, 104, 105, 106, 107-9, 120, 122, 128, 131, 132, 133, 134, 135, 137-41, 143, 146-48
Hawtrey, Sir Ralph, 10
Heller, Walter W., 117
Hinshaw, Randall, 1-9, 10, 67-69, 95, 129, 130
Housman, A. E., 13
Hume, David, 13, 48, 103

Jamison, Conrad C., 88
Johnson, Harry G., 12, 71
Johnson, President Lyndon B., 3, 7
Jones, Aubrey, 140

Kant, Immanuel, 57, 58
Kennedy, President John F., 3
Keynes, Lord, 10, 49, 121, 123, 126-27
Kindleberger, Charles P., 92

McClellan, H. C., 99-102, 103, 104, 131
Machlup, Fritz, 2, 4, 5, 9, 11, 15, 26-37, 39, 46, 48, 63, 64, 74, 75-76, 81, 82, 83, 86-88, 89-91, 93, 94, 95, 97, 107-9, 110, 118-19, 129, 130, 136, 137, 143, 148
Magnifico, Giovanni, 35-36, 65, 79-80, 117-18
Marshall, Alfred, 121, 125
Martin, William McChesney, Jr., 94
Meany, George, 99, 100
Mill, John Stuart, 125-26
Mises, Ludwig von, 122

159

SUBJECT INDEX